Mba Mbulu's
AN INTRODUCTION TO
WHITE HISTORY:
The History of White America

ISBN 1-883885-22-1 LCIP Pending

[United States History: Colonial thru 1877; Black History, Native Americans, Washitaw, Revolutionary War, African slavery and slave trade, westward expansion, secession, War Between the States, Reconstruction]

A Production of
ASET Publications
P.O. Box 60033
Washington, DC 20039

You can take this and many other Black Studies courses
free of charge on the internet at
www.asetbooks.com.
Learn what some people don't want you to know!

"*One*

Rotten

Apple

Spoils

The

Barrel"

PREFACE

MBA MBULU'S AN INTRODUCTION TO WHITE HISTORY: The History of White America, is a summary of the concepts, principles and motivating factors that led to the establishment and expansion of the United States of America. Since it is usually implied that "American" history is the history of (superior) white people, this precise title makes it clear that such is not the case. There are several histories that make up American history, and the history of white people is played out by the same ordinary human beings on the same ordinary stages as that of Black, African-American or Native American history.

What MBA MBULU'S AN INTRODUCTION TO WHITE HISTORY brings to the forefront is the unusually concentrated role that finances and the profit motive have played in white history; that is, in the political and social development of white America. It is white Americans' unusual preoccupation with finances and profits that distinguishes them and their institutions from those of all other Americans. And it behooves all other Americans to not underestimate that unusual preoccupation when determining the essence of their relations with white America.

One can acquire a more complete basis for understanding the underlying principles that guide this writng by reading Chapter One of TEN LESSONS: AN INTRODUCTION TO BLACK HISTORY (Mba Mbulu). To learn about the specific events discussed in this book, one can read almost any American History book. How these events are interpreted in this book is based on my intensive research and time tested understanding of the factors that have traditionally motivated the United States of America, particularly its leadership.

There are several specific titles that can help students get a more objective understanding of American history than is usually provided. These titles include (but are not limited to):

BLACK RECONSTRUCTION IN AMERICA W. E. B. DuBois
JOHN BROWN W. E. B. DuBois
THEY CAME BEFORE COLUMBUS Ivan Van Certima

SLAVERY AND THE FOUNDERS: Race and Liberty in the Age of Jefferson Paul Finkelman

BURY MY HEART AT WOUNDED KNEE Dee Brown

WILDERNESS AT DAWN Ted Morgan

THE BLACK BOOK Middleton A. Harris

LEXINGTON AND CONCORD: The Beginning of the War of the American Revolution Arthur Tourtellot

THE GREAT EXPERIMENT: George Washington and the American Republic John Rhodehamel

THE REPUBLIC OF LETTERS James Morton Smith

TEN LESSONS: AN INTRODUCTION TO BLACK HISTORY Mba Mbulu

THE LONG BITTER TRAIL: Andrew Jackson and the Indians Anthony Wallace

THE AGE OF CAPITAL E. J. Hobsbawm

To all people, so that We might have a more complete basis for gaining understanding and applying what we have learned. Mba Mbulu

TABLE OF CONTENTS

Section One: WHITE AMERICA'S ROOTS

1: Cristobal Colon 10
2: The Spanish Armada 11
3: White America's Founding Fathers 11
4: Governments, Businessmen And Churches 12
5: Businessmen, Laborers And Malcontents 14
6: Peers And Peons 15
7: Education And Misinformation 17
Section One: Summary 19
Section One: Review Questions 21

Section Two: THE BRITISH COLONIES

8: Establishing A Colony 22
I. Perspectives on Established Boundaries 22
II. Perseverance and Social Contracts 24
III. Extending Boundaries 25

9: The English Colonies 26
I. Early Steps 26
II. Business, Business, Business 27
III. Colonization Initiatives 27
IV. Tobacco 28

10: Antagonisms Within The Colonies 30
I. Farmers, Planters and Tradesmen 30
II. Capitalism 30

11: Problems Between Mother And Child 36
Section Two: Summary 38
Section Two: Review Questions 39

Section 3: THE UNITED STATES OF AMERICA

12: The Discovery Of A New Land 41
13: The Colonies Become Prosperous 45
I. Slave Labor 45
II. Underpaid Labor 47
III. Money Crops, Money Products And Money Services 48
IV. Efficiency Of Operations 51

14: The Revolutionary War Period (1750 - 1783) 53

I. Colonial Discontentment 53
II. Pontiac's War 54
III. Sectional Incompatibilities 56

15: The Revolutionary War 59
I. The Business of War 59
II. The Burden of War 60
III. That's Why They Fight The War 63
IV. They Fight The War 65
V. Victory 68

16: The Articles Of Confederation (1781 - 1787) 70
I. Establishing A Provisional Government 70
II. The Articles of Confederation 73
III. The Articles of Confederation: Danger Signs 74

17: Life Under The Articles Of Confederation 78
I. Everyday People and Elites 78
II. Everyday People 79
III. Elites 80
IV. Seeds of Discontent 81
V. The Straws That Stirred The Milkshake 84
VI. The Industrial Revolution 85
VII. Adam Smith 87
VIII. Wall Street 88

18: The Overthrow Of The American Revolution 91
I. The Articles of Confederation (1781-1787) .. 91
II. Amending A Constitution 92
III. Some Business Men Meet 94
IV. A Constitutional Coup d'Etat (1787) 94
V. And States Rights??? 97
VI. A Pro-Slavery Law of the Land 99
Section Three: Summary 101
Section Three: Review Questions 102
Section 4: THE LAW OF THE LAND
19: A Nation Steeped In Hypocrisy 106
I. Introduction 106
II. Out With the Vanquished 106
III. Political Continuity 108
IV. A New Government 109

V. The Pillars of Hypocrisy 111

20: The Business Of The Nation 116
I. The Invisible Pilot 116
II. Office Holders and Policies 117
III. Political Parties 119
IV. From Issues to Non-Issues 120

21: The Nation Ages And Expands 123
I. America's Paradigm 123
II. Fair Weather Morals 123
III. Westward Expansion 124
IV. Native American Policy 130
V. Unpaid and Underpaid Labor 135
VI. Sectional Hostilities 138

22: War In America 142
I. White America Attacks Black People 142
II. Black People Defend Themselves 146

23: The War Between The States 154
I. The Beginning of War 154
II. Pretexts and Crutches 155
III. The War To Free The South 157
IV. They Fight The War 159
V. Where Does White Power Go From Here? 163

24: Reconstructing White Power 167
I. The Shot That Ended The War 167
II. Reconstruction: A False Start 170
III. Congress Takes Control 173
IV. The Reconstruction Amendments 176
V. Blood Is Always Thicker 178
Section Four: Summary 180
Section Four: Review Questions 181

CONCLUSION 186
I. Of Business, By Business, and For Business 186
II. Economic Capitalism, Political Capitalism And Social Capitalism ..... p. 187
III. And The Future? 189

Section One:
WHITE AMERICA'S ROOTS

CHAPTER ONE:
CRISTOBAL COLON

[Note: The man Americans call Christopher Columbus was born in Italy. His birth name was Cristoforo Colombo. The Spanish knew him as Cristobal Colon. Since history remembers him because of the trips he made under the auspices of the Spanish crown, the name Cristobal Colon is used in this book.]

In 1492, Cristobal Colon (Christopher Columbus) and 90 or so followers left Spain in search of a shorter route to the spices and riches of the East Indies. Cristobal Colon grossly miscalculated the route, bumped into a land mass that was unknown to Europeans and characteristically claimed not only ownership of the land (for the king and queen of Spain) but ownership of its inhabitants as well (the Arawaks and Tainos, whom he ignorantly called "Indians"). Cristobal Colon declared himself Governor of the land and established his headquarters on Hispaniola (Haiti and the Dominican Republic now make up that area). After observing the native inhabitants of the new land, he wrote that they were timid, loving, giving people who had no iron, steel or weapons. After noting that the manners of the Native Americans were superior to those of the Europeans, Cristobal Colon immediately began planning to work them to death, torture them, murder them, starve them, expose them to deadly European diseases and destroy their way of life. It is here, in Cristobal Colon's fortuitous "discovery," characteristic greed and arrogance, lack of concern for the rights of others and ruthless cruelty that the history of the United States of America begins.

CHAPTER TWO:
THE SPANISH ARMADA

In 1588, nearly 100 years after Cristobal Colon accidentally "discovered" the "new world," England defeated Spain in a war for control of Europe's seas. During this war the Spanish Armada (navy), the source of Spain's military power, was practically destroyed, and England emerged as a European power. England's defeat of the Spanish Armada put the recently emerged question of who would dominate the new land in substantial doubt. The wealth and energy of the elite classes in several European countries, their general affluence and relationship to their respective "government" and the military might of the respective armed forces were to eventually determine what countries would control what parts of the "new world," and under what conditions.

CHAPTER THREE:
WHITE AMERICA'S FOUNDING FATHERS

The United States of America is dominated by three major European strands; those of France, Germany and Great Britain/England. White America's founding fathers, as early as the late 1600s, were concerned about the rights of the common man, but not nearly as concerned as the French masses. White America's founding fathers were also concerned about being efficient and applying themselves diligently, and much like the seed of Germany's elite, they preferred to receive the profits generated by the efficiency and diligence of poorly compensated laborers. And, white America's founding fathers were concerned about making money, as much money as possible! Incredibly, white America's founding fathers were more concerned about this than any of the British financiers from whom they took their cue. These three elements, (1) a little bit of concern about the common person, (2) more concern about efficiency and the diligent application of poorly compensated laborers and (3) a whole mountain of concern about making money; these three elements were fortuitously blended into a hybrid

economic-centric status quo. The result: A business oriented political structure (political capitalism) that catered
to relatively small numbers of "elite" individuals and undermined a golden opportunity to establish a white power
democracy that would have benefitted the masses of its
whites citizens.

White America's founding fathers were one rotten
apple in what could have been a relatively fine American
barrel. But that rotten apple spoiled America's barrel and
ruined whatever chance the United States had of achiev-
ing greatness. Instead, what the United States became
was a rich country (financially speaking), but the price
its citizens and humanity had to pay, and continue to
pay, is staggering.

CHAPTER FOUR:
GOVERNMENTS, BUSINESSMEN AND CHURCHES

Cristobal Colon's "discovery" of a new land stirred
the energies of European governments (kings and
queens), individuals and churches. European governments
were interested in how they could profit financially from
the discovery, and how they could use the discovery to
increase their military might and decrease that of their
ever menacing and belligerent neighbors. The three major European powers of the time, England, France and
Spain, proved to be the most capable of the lot. In Spain
and France, the crowns (government) generally took direct control of the exploratory initiatives, with assistance
from individuals of means and affluence who imagined
that considerable profits could somehow be made. In
England, a somewhat different approach was taken. For
the most part, the English crown did not directly participate in exploratory ventures, opting instead to encour-
age English merchants and entrepreneurs to spearhead
those initiatives. In all cases, be they English, French,
Spanish or Dutch, the attempts at settlement in the new
land were, first and foremost, economic ventures.

It is important that the reader understand what was
just said. Each English settlement or colony, at its core,

was a business establishment. In essence, the colonies that were to become the United States of America started off as little businesses; as individual proprietorships, partnerships and corporations. Businesses do not hinge on democratic principles, nor are they concerned about creating environments that promote equality and justice. By understanding this, students of United States history can see how they have been deliberately or haphazardly misled by traditional historians of United States history. Traditional historians speak of the American colonies as if they were political units that carried out all of the economic functions that political units must carry out in order to survive. In fact, the American colonies were business units that carried out all of the non-business functions (including the legal and political ones) a business must carry out in order to survive.

Also, understand the implications of the English crown encouraging businesses to take the lead in the exploration and settlement of colonies in the new land. The English, the ones who prevailed in the areas of the new land that became known as the United States of America, firmly believed in the philosophy of "let business pave the way," and passed that philosophy on to the whites who settled this land. The whites who settled this land, in turn, passed that philosophy down to succeeding generations of "Americans." On the whole, "Americans" have proved themselves incapable of objectively analyzing that philosophy and determining if it is indeed best for business to lead the way when a social structure is supposed to be "of the people, by the people and for the people."

Business was also at the core of the church's interest in the new world and its native inhabitants. Better than any other institution, the church was able to (1) take advantage of an individual's ignorance of the unknown and (2) camouflage its primary objective of accumulating wealth. The collection of tithes, taxes and titles to land generated huge sums of income for the church, and plenty of each could be obtained from the natives and settlers of the new land. Additionally, the church's ideology was more consistent, comprehensive and long standing than any of the business and political ideologies of the time, and that tended to give the church a greater aura of legitimacy than the others. In the new land, the church saw the opportunity to not only maintain but increase its flow of wealth and influence, and if push came to shove, it was willing to butt heads with businesses and governments to do so. However, since the church did not have an independent army that could force its will in the case of a dramatic confrontation, it preferred to work hand in hand with "the government." This it did quite effectively in the Americas.

In summary, one must remember that, like all businesses, the American colonies were established to generate revenue and provide sources of income for those parties that invested in them. The American colonies were not established to promote human justice and champion the rights of everyday people. The American colonies were established to make money. This is critical to understanding the energy that motivated many colonial patriots during the American Revolutionary War period, why that energy clashed with that of the individuals who became known as America's founding fathers, and why white America's founding fathers were able to prevail.

CHAPTER FIVE:
BUSINESSMEN, LABORERS AND MALCONTENTS

The early Englishmen who were interested in the new land can be split into two essential types: (1) those who had managed to thrive to a larger or smaller degree at home and had no intention of leaving Europe and (2) those who had failed miserably. The type that had failed miserably can be split into two general groups: (1) those who saw the new land as a new chance for them to make something worthwhile of their lives and (2) those malcontents and dregs of society who were either fed up with English political, social and "religious" restraints or forced to go to the new land because the English crown and "elite" wanted to be free of their presence. The first type, the merchants, looked at the new land as they would have looked at any business opportunity. The second type, the failures and malcontents, looked at the new land as unemployed individuals looked at new employment opportunities, as prison inmates looked at an impending transfer, and as ideological activists looked at the opportunity to establish and live in a socio-political environment that is more to their liking. The two types had little or no genuine interest in each other as human beings. They were simply parties to a risky business venture that promised little of known quality or quantity. They were employers and employees, owners and workers, methodical businessmen and random laborers; and all that those designations implied. They ventured into the same arena of economic possibilities, but from different doors that opened to different realities and introduced different risks. They were not enemies, at least not in the traditional understanding of the term, but they very well could have been. In fact they SHOULD have been, WOULD have been- - if the laborers and malcontents had been as organized and methodical, and as systematic and calculating as their merchant counterparts.

If the laborers and malcontents had been as organized and methodical, and as systematic and calculating as their merchant counterparts, the gains made by the unknown patriots during the American Revolutionary War period might have been sustained, and the United States might have become a nation that actually championed humankind. But, when one introduces the term "if" in a historical context, it indicates the prevalence of a failure or shortcoming. Thus, those who could have made the United States great were not equipped to resist those who were bent on making the United States rich. The rest, as has been said so often by so many, is history.

CHAPTER SIX:
PEERS AND PEONS
European society has never been a society of equals. The royal families and merchants who were interested in

the settling of the new land had convinced themselves that they were better than most other human beings, and they acted accordingly. Most of the laborers who were to actually travel to the new land, settle there and help establish the colonies had been convinced that some persons were better than they were, and they acted accordingly. Thus, a tradition and mindset of peers (upper class humans) and peons (lower class humans) arrived in the new land with the settlers, the merchants and the merchants' blueprints. As soon as the settlers proved themselves incapable of breaking with that tradition and mindset, the new land was doomed to become a social offspring of the old world (Europe).

It is important to recognize that this tradition of peers and peons was believed in by both those who benefitted from it ("peers") and those who were victimized by it ("peons"). This is indicative of the paradoxes and seeming contradictions that have historically rendered Europe's white masses incapable of effectively rebelling against the white elites who abuse them. Even as they knew they were being abused, Europe's white masses believed in the legitimacy of the system that abused them, and looked up to most of the individuals who were the architects of their abuse. Even as they knew "the law" was corrupt and unjust, Europe's masses believed in the legitimacy of "the law" and the authority of those individuals who enacted or proclaimed unjust laws. And even as they knew they were being robbed of the fruits of their labor, Europe's masses believed in the legitimacy of the economic/political system that facilitated their robbery, and admired those individuals who accumulated wealth as a result of their robbery. In order to make the new land a different world, the settlers of the colonies would have to effectively disconnect from Europe's tradition of peers and peons. Since the mindset and self-defeating quality that hindered Europe's masses was passed on to the white Europeans who crossed the Atlantic Ocean to settle in the new world, the settlers would prove themselves incapable of disconnecting to the necessary degree.

The settling of the new land proved that Europeans can be taken out of Europe, but Europe can't be taken out of Europeans. The disconnections the colonial settlers needed to make in order to disable the allegiances they held for Europe's traditions were of a too fundamental nature. Europe's traditions were so dear to the settlers of the new land that they were incapable of objectively characterizing or assessing many of them, much less disavowing their legitimacy. America was a new land to Europeans, but the differences between the European colonies and Europe were to be kept to the most functional minimum.

CHAPTER SEVEN:
EDUCATION AND MISINFORMATION

The information that Europe's elites possessed and had access to was the type that is useful to long range planners and doers. As a result, Europe's elite groups, including the church, merchants and crown, were able to establish status quos and initiate processes that could keep those status quos strong and viable. On the other hand, the information that Europe's poor and working people possessed was the type that could only get them from one shortsighted day to the next. Europe's poor and working people were not able to establish a status quo that systematically acted in their interests, nor were they able to consistently create conditions that Europe's crowns, businesses and churches feared enough to accommodate. This widely disproportionate quality and use of information ensured that Europe's elites would always be dictating terms, and Europe's poor and working people would always be reacting and adjusting to the terms dictated by Europe's peers. This would have to change if the new land were to become something other than a replica of the old country.

But there were serious barriers to bringing about this change. To begin with, the individuals who made up Europe's masses were not impressed with each other's learning, which they all too often mistook for intelligence. For the most part, Europe's working people were convinced that Europe's peers were smarter and more intelligent than they were, and that they were unable to absorb, process and utilize data as efficiently as Europe's peers. This was not a conclusion that Europe's masses had haphazardly settled into, it was what Europe's elite had crammed into the minds of poor and working people for centuries and centuries. Unfortunately, Europe's masses did not effectively realize that.

Additionally, the views of those peons who resisted the ideological pomp and circumstance of the peers were, for various reasons, either never written or, if written, rarely published, promoted or publicly discussed on a grand scale. Thus, Europe's masses got very little opportunity, relatively speaking, to entertain ideas and trains of thought that were markedly contrary to those passed down to them by Europe's elites. By entertaining widely divergent thoughts, Europe's masses, over a period of time, could have created an independent body of ideological and functional realities. These realities, which gradually would have assumed an aura of legitimacy, could have impacted on Europe's masses when they needed to act in their own interests or protect themselves against the intrigues of Europe's peers. They could have, but they didn't because Europe's elites did everything (moral and immoral) within their power to limit the range of thought of the masses.

Thirdly, because Europe's masses had been schooled to value information that sprung from among Europe's peers and served the interests of Europe's peers, the ideas of independent minded peons tended to meet resistance among the masses and be looked at suspiciously. As such, the ideas of independent minded peons were instinctively assumed to be less than legitimate. When an elitist spoke in the interest of elites, the masses assumed that he spoke in good faith, and the burden was on his detractors to disprove what he had said. In contrast, when a "peon" spoke in the interest of peons, the masses assumed that he spoke with malicious intent, and the burden was on him to prove that what he said was in good faith. When one understands the psychological implications of those assumptions, one realizes the huge political disadvantage Europe's masses passed on to the majority of the white individuals who were to settle the new land.

Information and misinformation can run hand in hand. Information that promotes the interests of a peer group becomes misinformation if it is deliberately passed on to "peons" in a context that encourages the peons to not act in their own interests. And, just as the knowledge and ignorance of a rich and powerful person or group is much more dangerous than that of the average citizen, knowledge passed on by institutions that are controlled by a rich and powerful group are exponentially more forceful than knowledge passed on by an independent individual. Europe's peers systematically used their institutions to rate and assign value to all classes of information and information givers, and succeeded in getting Europe's peons to accept their ratings and value assignments. As a consequence, Europe's peers were able to define what constitutes "good" learning, establish "educational" objectives for Europe's masses that were predicated on the needs of Europe's peers, and manipulate Europe's masses into believing in and developing an allegiance to the mythology of the white elite. A white mass of people that believed in and had an allegiance to the white mythology is critically important to understanding the development of the English colonies, and it can not be overemphasized.

Section One: Summary

The "discovery" of America by Cristobal Colon initiated a series of fortuitous (unintended or "lucky") developments that resulted in the formation of the United States of America. This fortuitous element has reared its head many times, and has played more than a negligible role in many of white America's successes. History tells researchers that luck tends to run out sooner or later, so those American power players who are intent on initiating fundamental changes have history on their side. However, alongside that element of luck are the deliberately laid pillars of greed, arrogance, lack of concern for the rights of others and ruthless cruelty. White America will not run away from those pillars, so the power players who are intent on initiating fundamental changes have to conduct their struggle in a manner that de-legitimizes and de-constructs those pillars.

Those pillars are deeply entrenched. The elite classes in Europe, with their snobbish attitudes and ideologies, were pivotal to the exploration of the new world. European governments, businessmen and churches, all masters of greed, arrogance and hypocrisy, were responsible for settling the little businesses that became the American colonies. Europe's peers and peons, advocates and functionaries of social inequality, traveled to the new world and took on the roles of colonial businessmen, laborers and malcontents who had little or no genuine interest in each other as human beings. They, in turn, evolved into white America's founding fathers, possessors of a little bit of concern about the common person, more concern about efficiency and diligence of unpaid and poorly paid laborers and a whole mountain of concern about making money. The result: A business oriented political structure (political capitalism) that catered to relatively small numbers of "elite" individuals and effectively ignored the well being of the masses.

Those who could have made the United States great were not equipped to resist those who were bent on making the United States rich. The information that white elites possessed and had access to was the type that is useful to long range planners and doers. On the other hand, the information that white poor and working people possessed was the type that could only get them from one shortsighted day to the next. With the objective of making the United States rich, white elites educated themselves and seized control of the education process. This enabled them to miseducate white America's peons and render them incapable of establishing an America that was of the people, by the people and for the people.

Section One: Review Questions

(1) Did Cristobal Colon think that the people who occupied the new land were savages?

(2) Did Cristobal Colon think that the manners of the people who occupied the new land were superior to those of Europeans?

(3) Why did Cristobal Colon decide to enslave the people who occupied the new land?

(4) What roles did Europe's elite play in the development of the new land?

(5) Why are white America's founding fathers referred to as one rotten apple?

(6) What were the two major concerns of white America's founding fathers?

(7) What did governments, businessmen and churches have in common in the development of the new land?

(8) "Each English settlement or colony, at its core, was a business establishment." What is the importance of that statement?

(9) What was the relationship of businessmen, laborers and malcontents in the development of the new land?

(10) Explain the following statement: "Those who could have made the United States great were not equipped to resist those who were bent on making the United States rich."

(11) What is a peer? What is a peon? What is the relevance of peers and peons to the development of the new land?

(12) What role did education and misinformation play in the development of the new land?

Section Two:
THE BRITISH COLONIES

It is here, in Cristobal Colon's fortuitous "discovery," characteristic greed and arrogance, lack of concern for the rights of others and ruthless cruelty that the history of the United States of America begins.

CHAPTER EIGHT:
ESTABLISHING A COLONY

I. Perspectives on Established Boundaries

The major difference between individuals and societies has nothing to do with race, intelligence or other such factors. The major difference between individuals and societies revolves around their willingness to manipulate a status quo or go beyond the boundaries or parameters established by a status quo. Those who insist on going beyond the established boundaries become pioneers, leaders and peers, and sometimes martyrs. Those who are content with remaining within the established boundaries become followers, sycophants, peons and victims.

If nothing else, white America's colonizers and founding fathers were big time gamblers who were willing to stretch the boundaries to the limit. The status quo that prevailed in Europe on the eve of the settlement of the new land was their status quo, and they manipulated it to the max. But the land that Cristobal Colon had recently "discovered" was beyond their zone of control, so they had to gamble in order to profit from it. They gambled when they drew up and notarized deeds of ownership to a land mass that they did not own. They gambled when they decided to establish businesses in a faraway land that they were not familiar with. They gambled when they repeatedly paid to send malcontents, criminals and other dregs of European society across 3000 miles of ocean in floating death traps to settle the new land. They gambled that they would be able to keep the settlements supplied with goods and necessities until the settlers could produce enough goods and services to support themselves. Native Americans could have practically destroyed their chances of success by killing the settlers en masse every time a ship came to the shores of the new land, but white America's founding fathers gambled that the Native Americans would be too civilized and unsuspecting to do so. And white America's founding fathers gambled that, once they got a foothold established, they would be able to seize control of sections of the new land mass, de-populate those sections of its native inhabitants and re-populate them with individuals of their choosing. They gambled they could stretch the odds to the absolute limit and succeed with the right combination of good fortune and ruthlessness (which they called "God"). If in the end they realized they were not going to get their way, they gambled that they could dodge enough arrows to make a clean getaway or, if creased by a few, recuperate, learn from their miscalculations and move on to their next project.

They gambled! White America's colonizers and founding fathers took a huge gamble, and it is to their credit that they were willing to do so. Even though most of the white investors and merchants did not succeed, their gamble succeeded, and it was the gamble that meant more than anything else. It was the gamble that made the nascent businesses and colonies in the new land possible, it was the gamble that allowed those nascent businesses and colonies to evolve into profitable corporations and states, and it was the gamble that gave eventuality to what is now called the United States of America. White America's colonizers and founding fathers gambled, and there is much that an abused people can learn from that.

Not only did white America's founding fathers gamble, they persevered. They were able to persevere for the same reason they were willing to gamble-- their vision of what they had to gain was much more powerful than their fear of the risks that were involved. Unfortunately

for humanity, their vision was of individual riches and profits, not the making of a better world for people in general. As the new land evolved into the United States of
America, the vision of white America's colonizers and
founding fathers took strong root and rendered a myriad
of more integral visions blurry and inconsequential.

II. Perseverance and Social Contracts

The men who began the process of colonizing the
new land were not the same as those who completed
that process. More than 100 years of exploring empires
and establishing outposts had been engaged in by Europeans before English settlers disembarked and established
the first English settlement that was to survive in the
new land. Several failures preceded the settling of
Jamestown, Virginia in 1607, and each failure was dearly
felt. But neither of the failures caused the early colonizers to lose sight of their objective. They persevered, and
that is why, by the early 1730s, permanent English settlements stretched along the Atlantic coast from what is
now the state of New Hampshire to that of Georgia. By
the 1730s, each of these settlements, each of these
individual and group proprietorships, had been organized
into political units. Within another 40 year period, these
businesses in the guise of political units were to evolve
from colonial status to independent states, and declare
the birth of the United States of America.

Much is made of the social contracts, the agreements
among the settlers in colony after colony, that were
agreed upon during this early time period; the Mayflower
Compact being an example. In fact, there was no social
contract that either sought the involvement of or was
meant to benefit the masses of the people who were to
settle the colonies or the new land as a whole. The social
contracts and forms of political organization that were
established were agreements among certain white men
that were designed to disproportionately benefit their
small group. They were based, for the most part, on the

English Magna Carta, which was an elitist-centric agreement between businessmen (barons, church leaders, etc.) and the king of England. Like the Magna Carta, the social contracts that the settlers entered into were spurred mostly by money matters, and they made it easier for elitist-minded individuals to relate to and interact with each other in a somewhat civil climate. These social contracts were not documents that proposed or confirmed the equality of all people. As a matter of fact, at the time of the settling of the new land, equality was as far away from the minds of the English colonizers as it was from the minds of King John and the merchants who agreed to the Magna Carta nearly 400 years earlier.

More will be mentioned on the Magna Carta and related "contracts" (forms of government) later, particularly when we discuss the U. S. constitution. We need to pay a great deal of attention to them because they demonstrate that the governments that were established by the early settlers and colonizers lacked legitimacy. Since the masses of the people in the colonies were not allowed to play a part in the process that created the governments, they were not bound by the dictates and laws enacted by those governments. If the settlers who populated the new land in the beginning had been able to reason as such and organize effectively, the development of the United States of America would have been markedly different.

III. Extending Boundaries

At times, those who prefer to stretch the boundaries have reason on their side. At other times, that is true of those who prefer to remain within established parameters. Unfortunately, who is right or wrong at a given moment or during a given dispute is not the key to determining whether or not something worthwhile will be accomplished. All too often, that key is the frame of mind and/or belief system of the various participants in the process.

CHAPTER NINE:
THE ENGLISH COLONIES

I. Early Steps

The first step in the establishment of businesses and colonies in the new land was settling the area with as many white people as possible. Once that was achieved, the early English colonizers proceeded to stage two of the process; the elimination of the new land's native population. The English settlers took to this task with a passion, so much so that, barely three years after the settlers arrived in Jamestown in 1607, Native Americans were being systematically attacked and murdered by soldiers and armed bands of white individuals. Native Americans were victims of repeated mass poisonings, their canoes and fishing boats were destroyed in order to hamper their efforts to feed themselves, and their villages and crops were burned to the ground. In many areas, murdering Native Americans became a business, a quite profitable one, and many settlements awarded a bounty for each scalp of a dead "injun" a settler produced. Probably suffering from a state of shock and being unable to comprehend what was actually happening to them (they had never been confronted with this type of behavior or mentality before), the Native American was unable to react quickly enough to save himself or his land. For all intents and purposes, the Native American perished, and the ownership of the new land ended up in the hands of white people. [For an in depth explanation of why the Native Americans failed to maintain ownership of their land, see Lesson Two of my book, Ten Lessons: An Introduction to Black History]

Thus, the legacy of the Native Americans who treated the white settlers humanely, helped them survive and refused to "fight hate with hate" is the physical decimation of the Native American and the destruction of their way of life. Some historians have estimated that as many as 100 million Native Americans were killed by the whites who settled the new world. One can only wonder how many deaths would have been avoided and how much suffering would have been precluded if the kindhearted and self-serving [but short sighted and self-defeating] acts carried out by "good" Native Americans like Squanto, Samoset, Powhatan and Pocahontas had never been done.

II. Business, Business, Business

As I stated earlier, what became the United States of America began as several business endeavors. If one analyzes each of the reasons for England's colonization efforts, business concerns will be found at their root. (1) England's "overpopulation" was a financial liability: hungry, unproductive, unemployed and homeless people taxed England's government, business entities and social institutions. (2) England was a hotbed of wool production; new markets would provide more users and purchasers of wool, and more revenue. (3) England was also in serious need of precious metals, spices, condiments and medicinal herbs; new settlements would provide more producers of many of those items.

As for the religious reasons given for the colonization of the new land, they sounded good but, when put to a serious test, did not have the substance to stand on their own merit. As I stated earlier, the church was the most adept institution at camouflaging its true objectives. Religious conversion and religious doctrines were code names for collecting money. Indeed, the church was more interested in and adept at collecting money than anything else.

III. Colonization Initiatives

So the English invested in colonization initiatives in earnest. The first permanent colony was founded in 1607 in Jamestown, Virginia. As it were, the colony of Jamestown barely survived. Half a year after the first settlers arrived, half were dead and the rest would have been unable to save themselves if the Native Americans had decided to eliminate them. Captain John Smith's friendship with and marriage to Pocahontas probably helped keep the Native Americans in the Jamestown area from making a crushing attack against the whites. That, in turn, allowed the whites to bide their time as they built up their numbers and planned their campaign of genocide against the Natives. For a brief period of a few years, the destiny of the whites was, for all intents and purposes, completely out of their hands, and they realized that. All they could do was keep on struggling to survive and hope for the best. Fortuitous circumstances had resulted in Cristobal Colon discovering this new land. Perhaps luck would continue to be on their side.

IV. Tobacco

Those who are afraid to march against the obstacles they will have to overcome are of little use to a serious economic or political endeavor. The white colonizers and settlers of the new land were not afraid, and they were rewarded for their valor. What the owners of Jamestown needed more than anything else, with the exception of more luck, was a profitable business activity. A locally grown crop, tobacco, proved to be an answer to their prayers. Beginning around 1613, the colonizers began exporting tobacco to England, and the profits began to increase exponentially. Tobacco became what is known as a money crop, and this single economic asset enabled the colony of Jamestown to overcome many of its weaknesses. Because of tobacco, it became possible for many of the settlers to become private owners of property. This made those who were in the new land more interested in staying, and attracted other Europeans who, otherwise, would not have been interested in making that trip across the Atlantic Ocean. Also, once tobacco became a money crop, more women saw an advantage in coming to the new land and more male settlers were able to purchase spouses and start families. The presence of a good number of women, in and of itself, added a sense of stability to the colonies that can not be overemphasized.

In spite of its new found prosperity, the colony of Jamestown could have been destroyed if the Red Native American had resolved to do so. They dealt serious blows to the invaders of their land several times, in Jamestown and the colonies to the north, but they could not conceive of what they needed to do to complete the job. It is to their credit and high level of development that they were not acquainted with that type of warfare. Unfortunately, those admirable qualities-- their civility and high level of development-- made it easier for the Europeans to eliminate them.

CHAPTER TEN:
ANTAGONISMS WITHIN THE COLONIES

I. Farmers, Planters and Tradesmen

For the most part, the English colonies were composed of farmers and planters. Complementing them were various commercial interests that revolved around maritime activities. More important than the different types of colonies were the types of labor systems employed and the different methods used by the settlers to organize the means of production and share the wealth that was generated. These differences were to stand out in the colonies during the pre-revolutionary period and plague the new nation for over 100 years.

The colonies in New England were characterized by agriculture, various types of fishing, shipbuilding and smaller industries that produced textiles, household goods and ironworks. By far the most profitable industry in this area was the liquor industry, augmented by the role New Englanders played in the molasses, rum and slave trade triangle. In the areas of New York, New Jersey and Pennsylvania, farming activities were complemented by the production of various textiles and the trading of furs. In the South, agriculture was nearly everything. Unique to the South was the appearance of and dependence on money crops such as tobacco, rice, indigo and, later, cotton. The South also had small lumber, textile and fur trading industries, but these complementary industries played a much smaller role in the economy of the South than in the other areas.

II. Capitalism

Who knows how old capitalism is, or where its initial roots took hold. It cannot be much younger than the trade guilds that cropped up throughout Europe as the so-called Dark Ages faded (circa 1000 A.D.). Wherever its roots might lay, capitalism matured in England sooner than the other major nations of Europe, and became an integral part of England's commercial status quo. In fact, one could make the argument that elements of capitalism were at the root of the chasm between King John and the elite classes of England that resulted in the issuance of the Magna Carta in 1215.

By the end of the 1200s, England's landowning classes had started aping England's merchants by demanding that rents be paid to them in cash rather than products. Following the lead of the landowners, farm laborers began demanding payment in cash also, and used their wages to move away from the rural areas if they saw fit. Those who moved away joined with other laborers in the urban areas and watched delightfully as labor shortages enabled laborers to demand higher and higher wages. Add to this the machinations of the benefactors of a thriving wool industry, and one begins to clearly see the influence of capitalistic activities on England's economic modus operandi.

England's wool industry prompted many of England's business minded individuals to break with the traditional economic concepts in regard to land. As a result, England's elites, in an effort to get more grazing land and maximize the production of wool, tried to rid the peasants of the little land they had (provoking revolts of the type led by Wat Tyler in the 1300s). This led to a rethinking and remaking of the concepts of labor, production, compensation and resource management (actually it was mismanagement) by England's commercial leaders. Thus, England's commercial status quo had begun to entertain and dance to a new economic beat while most of the rest of Europe remained tied to Europe's traditional economic values and practices.

By the time colonization had begun in the new land, England's people had been experiencing capitalism for in excess of 200 years. In fact, they were a capitalist minded lot, and they brought this taste for capitalism with them to the new land. Quite naturally, the English subjects who settled in the northern areas approached the issue of economics from a capitalist perspective. [Since much of the north, particularly New York, was initially colonized by the Dutch, and since the Dutch had capitalist roots that exceeded those of even England, the English taste for capitalism was expanded by the Dutch settlers they encountered.] Similarly, the English subjects who settled in the the middle areas approached the issue of economics from a capitalist perspective. And, the English subjects who settled in the southern areas approached the issue of economics from a capitalist perspective. The capitalist solutions arrived at by those in the northern and middle areas were similar enough that they could be merged without generating much ado. However, the capitalist solution arrived at by those settlers who occupied the southern areas was so different from the others that it strained the ability of the sections to get along harmoniously. This difference hovered for a seeming eternity, and threatened the creation of the United States of America during the Revolutionary War period. Later, this difference brought the country to the brink of civil war in the 1820s and, finally, exploded into bloody hostilities between the states in the 1860s. We will develop this theme more in later pages of this book.

The major problem generated by the different capitalist systems revolved around labor. For the most part, large and small farmers and businessmen in the northern and middle colonies in the early 1600s either worked for themselves or paid laborers to work for them. In the southern colonies, laborers were, for the most part, forced to work for free. From the point of view of those in the North, forced unpaid labor was detrimental for several reasons, including but not limited to the following: (1) Paid laborers increased the size of the consumer market and resulted in the healthy expansion of capitalism. Unpaid laborers, on the other hand, tended to stifle the growth of economic markets; (2) Paid laborers forced businessmen to adopt efficient business practices. Unpaid laborers, particularly in the agricultural sector, encouraged businessmen to lay waste to the most valuable resource of all--land (England's businessmen had learned from the experience of its wool industry); (3) Paid laborers tended to respect property and the rights of businessmen. Unpaid laborers tended to harbor grave resentments, disrespect law and order, destroy property and threaten the security of the entire nation; (4) Paid laborers tended to feel better about their prospects for the future, and were therefore more likely to feel a degree of contentment. By contrast, there was not the slightest degree of contentment among unpaid laborers; (5) Paid laborers could be "educated" and contribute not only to the economy, but to "society" at large. Unpaid laborers had to be kept uneducated and ignorant, and represented all of the dangers to society that lack of education and ignorance generally represent; (6) Paid labor was more likely to defend the status quo against foreign aggression, while the opposite was true for forced labor; and (7) Paid laborers tended to be healthier, less prone to fall victim to an epidemic and less likely to pose a health or sanitation threat to the overall community. The opposite was true of unpaid laborers. In short, then, what the Northern colonies saw when they looked at the southern areas was a form of capitalism that (1) restricted the growth and development of healthy, more profitable markets; (2) wasted resources that Northern businessmen could translate into millions of dollars in profit; (3) promoted disrespect for law and order; (4) decreased the value of property; (5) raised external security concerns and (6) raised internal security and sanitation concerns for the entire nation. Understanding this, one can see why Northern elites and business persons saw the Southern system of capitalism as a plague that should be eliminated. For various reasons, however, Northerners were obligated to tolerate the Southern system for as long as it possibly could.

Traditional historians make much of the fact that forced, unpaid labor was morally offensive, and assert that that motivated the North to seek the abolition of the Southern system. For the sake of humanity, we would want that to be the case, but the fact is otherwise. Northerners at no time, even during the Civil War, advocated the abolition of the Southern slave system. What Northern businessmen wanted to do was keep slavery from spreading to other parts of the country. If Northern and Southern businessmen could have agreed on that point, slavery would have been accepted as a permanent American economic institution. Thus, the disagreement between the Northern and Southern businessmen was not about the moral issue of slavery, but the spread of slavery. To both, slavery was strictly an economic issue.

If the settlers who populated the North had populated the South instead, it is likely that they would have been huge supporters of forced, unpaid labor. Therefore, it is safe to say that among the colonizers of the new land, morality had some substance, but only within relatively minor contexts. Certainly, making money was an activity that justified the trivialization of morality (as far as the moneymakers were concerned). For the colonizers, forced, unpaid labor could have been the worst sin imaginable, but if it were the key to a profitable industry or business, they would trivialize it and not give the matter a second thought. When it came to the things that mattered most to the colonizers and settlers of the new land, morality lost its substance and took its appropriate place in the back of their minds.

Traditional historians are truthful when they talk about the negative image unpaid, forced labor gave to all of the colonies and, later, the new nation. It generated a negative image, certainly, but an acceptable one. Those countries that made use of forced labor could be targeted and belittled by opponents of forced labor, but to little avail. Why? Because everybody knew forced, unpaid labor was wrong, but in the realm of human affairs, knowledge of right and wrong means little or nothing all too often. To value right more than wrong would have been better, but even that would not have guaranteed an end to an abusive labor system. What could have guaranteed that end? Only one thing: valuing right more than one values money and power. Even in the year 2000, white America is not civilized enough to accept that. The same was certainly true 250 years earlier.

CHAPTER ELEVEN:
PROBLEMS BETWEEN MOTHER AND CHILD

The mother country was Great Britain, and the child was the American colonies. The character of each was sufficiently lacking and the objectives of each were so essentially self-serving that any dispute between the two should have been considered par for the course. When the profit motive served as the basis of a dispute, the outbreak of violence should not only have been predictable, but expected.

The period that led up to the American Revolution was a period of discord between businessmen in the American colonies and money interested parties (government and business) in Great Britain. The everyday people in both areas were incidental to the hostilities that were evolving. Unfortunately, when the dispute exploded into war, everyday people took center stage, and bled and died for a cause that had little or nothing to do with their well-being.

Money was at the core of every dispute between Great Britain and the American colonies. In each and every issue, Great Britain was trying to either increase revenue by taxing the colonists or decrease expenditures by forcing the colonists to take on certain fiscal responsibilities. In each and every issue, the colonists were trying to either decrease their fiscal responsibilities or increase their share of the profits they earned. This contradiction began to reach critical mass when Pontiac, the chief of the Ottawa, took up arms in an attempt to drive the whites out of his territory. Even though Pontiac did not achieve his objectives, his response convinced the English that certain areas of the new land had to be set aside for the native Americans. The resulting Proclamation of 1763 restricted the areas that white settlers could move into and led to a frenzy of protests. By restricting the areas white settlers could move into, the British were restricting the ability of business-interested parties to expand into new markets, increase volumes of production and realize greater profits. The British were restricting the potential money sources of America's businessmen, and that was an economic sin.

Money was at the root of the Sugar, Currency, Stamp and Quartering Acts of 1764 and 1765. The British were trying to make the Americans assume more of their fair share of the tax burden, but the Americans were insisting that they were already being taxed excessively. Smartly, the American colonists did more than voice their disapproval; they also acted in a manner that made their convictions crystal clear. They organized defiant public demonstrations, partook of mob activities and terrorized tax collectors. One notable consequence of these defiant activities was the so-called Boston Massacre. The fact that British soldiers actually fired into a crowd of protesting colonists unified the colonies and made them aware of the need for them to be prepared to defend themselves against British aggressions.

The colonists also formed independent political bodies that represented their resolve to break with Great Britain if necessary. Great Britain was determined to make the colonies pay, one way or the other. The Tea Act (which was passed to save the British East India Company, a private business, from financial ruin) tried to force the colonists to buy tea from one company only. The colonists responded by refusing to drink tea and, in Boston, dumping shiploads of tea into the harbor. This led the crown to issue the so-called Intolerable Acts, which, in turn, led the colonists to form provisional governments called continental congresses. The First Continental Congress, formed in 1774, was composed of men who seemed intent on reconciliating with Great Britain. Sam Adams called them "half-way patriots," and John Adams was irate because they were reluctant to act with any independent conviction. However, when the Massachusetts Provincial Congress declared independence and formed a state army, the First Continental Congress had no choice but to act likewise. Great Britain could have relented and delayed the confrontation, but typically bundled up any chance it had of doing so. The road to the American Revolutionary War had been paved.

Traditional historians make it seem as if non-economic factors came into play that shifted the pendulum in one direction or the other. There were other factors at play, always, but these other factors were never so urgent that they dictated a course of action. Only the money factor was that powerful, and students of history should be aware of that reality. The fact that the everyday colonist resented British rule is beyond question, just as the fact that many colonists were looking for an opportunity to confront the redcoats "for once and for all." But these resentments would never have led to a confrontation of such magnitude as the American Revolution. Everyday people, though discontented, have a tendency to tolerate unjust conditions. Money interests, on the other hand, are so intent on getting their way that they will rub the flints until a spark is generated. Such is the stuff wars are made of.

Section Two: Summary

White America's colonizers and founding fathers were big time gamblers who were willing to stretch the boundaries to the limit. Not only were white America's founding fathers gamblers, they were perseverers. Once they set out to accomplish an objective, they stuck with it through the worst of times. They were able to persevere for the same reason they were willing to gamble-- their vision of what they had to gain was much stronger than their fear of what they stood to lose.

More important than the evolution of different types of colonies was the evolution of different types of labor systems in different section of the colonies. Morality had some substance, but only within a relatively minor context. In each of the sections, making money was what the colonizers were interested in. Forced, unpaid labor could have been the worst sin imaginable, but if it were the key to a profitable industry or business, morality would be trivialized and not given a second thought. When it came to the things that mattered most to the colonizers and settlers of the new land, morality lost its substance and took its appropriate place in the back of their minds.

Because the money interested parties in Great Britain and the American colonies were so much alike in too many undesirable ways, a serious disagreement between the two was only a matter of time. As the colonies became more and more profitable, the disagreements became more and more "intolerable" and explosive. Money was at the core of each of these disagreements, and money eventually led to the war that we call the American Revolution.

As cruel as it may seem, the legacy of the Native Americans who treated the white settlers humanely, helped them survive and refused to "fight hate with hate" Is the wholesale slaughter of their people and the destruction of the Native American's way of life. If the Native Americans had been more concerned about themselves and less concerned about people who were so different from them, they might have been able to protect their land, and the history of America might have followed a different path.

Section Two: Review Questions

(1) What does the author mean when he says white America's founding fathers were gamblers?

(2) Is it necessary for people to recognize the necessity of taking gambles if they aspire to accomplish grand objectives?

(3) What role did perseverance play in the development of the new land?

(4) What can a student of history learn from documents like the Mayflower Compact and the Magna Carta?

(5) What steps were involved in the settlement of the colonies?

(6) Were the native Americans who treated the white colonists humanely rewarded in kind?

(7) What is meant by the following statement: "Religious conversion and religious doctrines were code names for collecting money."

(8) Were the colonists "afraid to march against the obstacles?"

(9) Why didn't Native Americans systematically destroy Jamestown and other English colonies?

(10) What seeds of antagonism existed during the colonization period that set the stage for sectional animosities and the Civil War?

(11) Was liquor a profitable industry in the American colonies?

(12) What economic philosophy was practiced by the various colonial sections of the American colonies?

(13) Did the economic philosophy practiced by the various colonial sections of the American colonies manifest itself the same way everywhere?

(14) What role did labor play in the development of the American colonies?

(15) How did the capitalists in the North assess labor and delineate its pros and cons?

(16) What does the author mean when he says "making money was an activity that justified the trivialization of morality"?

(17) When the British enacted unfair tax laws, what did the colonists do to indicate that they were not going to submit to the English crown?

(18) What were continental congresses? Were the members of the continental congresses intent on breaking ties with Great Britain?

(19) Why is it unlikely that the resentments felt by everyday people would lead to a war for American independence?

Section 3:
THE UNITED STATES OF AMERICA

CHAPTER TWELVE:
THE DISCOVERY OF A NEW LAND

It is now generally conceded that Black People were the original people; that they were the original inhabitants of Africa and spread from there to other parts of the earth. One of the areas Black People migrated to prior to anyone else is America; North, Central and South. In those early days, long, long ago, the land and people were known as Washitaw.

Thus, the Washitaw were here to greet later migrators to the Americas. In North America, the Washitaw greeted migrators of Asian and Indo-European stock. The Washitaw, the native Blacks of the Americas, and Red People co-existed on a basis of equality and harmoniously, for the most part. The Washitaw lived a settled and highly civilized lifestyle; pyramids and mounds throughout the land became symbols of their presence, stability and culture. Red Americans were also highly civilized. While predominantly nomadic in some sections of North America, a large percentage of them chose a settled lifestyle. Naturally, there was a great deal of individual intercourse between members of the various groups. By the time white people arrived tens of thousands of years later, there were native American nations and individuals that were clearly Black, clearly Red and clearly a mixture of the two. The fact that sixth and seventh graders in America's schools are routinely misinformed about this is proof of how educationally inadequate America's schools are and how effectively they have been used as instruments of racial propaganda.

African people have known the world was round for tens of thousands of years; if there was any doubt, it was removed every time they looked at the round shadow of the earth on the moon. In spite of this, and in spite of his immense reliance on knowledge learned from African researchers, Herodotus (the white father of history- circa 450 BCE) still insisted that the earth was flat. More than 100 years after the time of Herodotus, Alexander the Great needed precise information about the earth for military reasons. His scientists concluded that the earth was round and provided supporting data. In spite of this, and quite characteristically, nearly 1500 years later modern day Europeans still were not convinced of the accuracy of that conclusion.

At the dawn of Europe's modern era, Europeans, in search of gold and spices, were obsessed with finding a shorter route to the Indies. One of the sailors at the forefront of this quest was Cristobal Colon. Cristobal Colon's geographical estimates were ridiculously erroneous, but his voyage based on those estimates ran him aground on a land mass that was unknown to Europeans. Cristobal Colon had "discovered" America.

Colon quickly noted that the people who occupied America had highly civilized manners, were timid and, most of all, did not practice war in the manner Europeans did. In short, they were unable to defend themselves against white aggression, so Colon immediately began to abuse them. After remaining in America for a short while, Colon kidnapped some of the native Americans, returned to Europe and laid out plans to invade America and enslave its native inhabitants.

When Colon and subsequent bands of Spanish invaders returned to the Americas, their policy of conquest and extermination was so brutal and complete that the Catholic Church intervened. However, instead of demanding that the abuse and extermination policy be terminated, the Catholic Church suggested that it be directed toward a different group of people. The Catholic Church was of the opinion that Black People from Africa were better equipped to do the labor that Europeans needed done and less human than the native Americans (so abusing and exterminating Blacks would be less of a crime in the "eyes of the Lord"). This practice of white power religions and white power governments conspiring to abuse people and decimate populations became a model that was followed by every European country that invested in the exploration of the new world.

Colon and the Spaniards devastated Central and South America, and the lower half of North America, including the southwest sections of the United States. They went as far north as Virginia, but were too overextended to make noticeable strides there. In the meantime, the English began to lay their claim and took control of the areas from Virginia northward. The English viewed the native Americans as savages, and their deliberate extermination was soon the accepted colonial policy.

As soon as the first permanent English colony was established in Jamestown (1607), the English colonists began to systematically wipe out the very people who had made their survival possible. The English attacked the Native Americans and killed them by the tens and twenties, and then hundreds, they deliberately exposed the natives to deadly diseases, they hatched plots to mass poison the natives and they destroyed the technology that enabled the natives to experience their traditional lifestyle. They destroyed canoes, foodstuffs, villages and buffaloes. The massacre of women and children was most effective, and a "scalp bounty" encouraged the participation of those colonists who might not have agreed with the policy. Just as colonizing the new world became a business, and just as slavery became a business, murdering native Americans became a business also. Such is the nature of what one finds rooted at the core of the United States of America.

If the natives of South America had known what the arrival of white people meant, they could have justifiably massacred the whites as they stepped onshore and changed the history of South America. If the natives of Central America had known what the arrival of white people meant, they could have justifiably massacred them as they stepped onshore and changed the history of Central America. And, if the natives of North America had known what the arrival of white people meant, they could have justifiably massacred the whites as soon as they stepped onshore and changed the history of North America. But the native Americans did not know, had no reason to even suspect. As a result, it was they who were unjustifiably massacred, practically exterminated and totally ridded of their land.

CHAPTER THIRTEEN:
THE COLONIES BECOME PROSPEROUS

I. Slave Labor

Business profitability revolves around three key factors: (1) cheap labor (2) a money crop, product or service and (3) efficiency of operations. Of the three, the first two produce far greater returns that the last. Let us briefly look at each and see how they contributed to the prosperity of the British colonies in America.

By the early 1600s, British colonists in the new world had benefitted from the unpaid labor they had wrenched from the native American population. While they exterminated Red and Black "Indians" in America, the whites simultaneously attacked, devastated and decimated Black nations in Africa. What were they searching for? They were searching for live human bodies to replace the unpaid laborers they had massacred. As a result, an entire nation of Blacks was robbed of its independence and equality, kidnapped, imported to the new land and widely dispersed to each and every colony. These unpaid laborers were called slaves, and their blood, sweat and tears made the American colonies rich.

By the 1750s, the wages the Blacks had earned but were never paid had landed in the pockets of white families all over the southern, northern and western sections of America. If the Blacks had been paid, the South still would have been profitable, but the profits would have been fairly divided and the benefits properly shared. Instead, all of the profits and benefits ended up in the pockets of white Southerners. If the Blacks had been paid, the North still would have been profitable, but the profits would have been fairly divided and the benefits properly shared. Instead, all of the profits and benefits ended up in the pockets of white Northerners. And, if the Blacks had been paid, the West still would have been profitable, but the profits would have been fairly divided and the benefits properly shared. Instead, all of the profits and benefits ended up in the pockets of white Westerners. More than any other factor, unpaid labor enabled white Americans to establish a cash flow, access to capital and a standard of living that far exceeded their smarts, business acumen and wildest economic dreams.

Trillions and trillions and trillions of dollars of unpaid wages went into the pockets of white businessmen and coffers of white local, state and federal governments. Trillions and trillions and trillions of dollars that could have supported Black institutions and Black independence and contributed to the development of the Black race helped construct white institutions and extend white power instead. Unpaid labor, more than any of the three factors mentioned earlier, is responsible for the development of what has become the United States of America.

But the white business people who invested in the new world were not interested in just any old unpaid labor. The white business people who invested in the new world wanted intelligent unpaid labor. They wanted highly civilized unpaid labor. They wanted experienced unpaid labor. They wanted unpaid labor that knew, better than white people, how to make the new world the best that it could be. White adventurers and mercenaries had been to Africa and seen a level of social organization that exceeded anything Europeans had ever managed to generate. They saw how advanced, knowledgeable and efficient African institutions were, and how democratically inclined and governable the African People were. They had also seen that Africans did not possess the weapons of destruction that Europeans possessed, nor practice war the way Europeans did. They therefore concluded, just as Cristobal Colon did about the natives of the new land, that the Africans would not be able to defend themselves against white military aggression. With little to no risk to themselves, the whites concluded, they could kidnap Blacks, acquire wealth by not paying them for their labor and use the extensive knowledge of the Blacks to build a nation that the whites were not knowledgeable enough to build on their own. What a bonanza!

II. Underpaid Labor

On the eve of the Revolutionary War, white business-men in the North had recognized that it was more advantageous and profitable to underpay laborers than to not pay them at all. By underpaying laborers, a labor system full of negative connotations and undertones could be removed and replaced with a different system, a "paid" system, that was almost as negative, but not nearly as familiar or identifiable. A paid labor system would enable business people to make grandiose moral, economic and social declarations that were misleading and deceptive. The picture of paid labor that was drawn up by Northern businessmen and their marketing experts made the public believe that the elimination of unpaid labor was the key to generating fair treatment for all laborers and returning respect to labor as an institution.

The system of paid labor sought by Northern businessmen was better for the worker than slavery (in ways), but it was not intended to get fair treatment for laborers or create respect for labor as an institution. This system of paid labor was meant to increase the profits of business people and reduce their sense of responsibility for the well being of their workers. With the system of paid labor sought by Northern businessmen, the laborer would be paid wages, and he was free to do whatever he wanted to do with those wages. If he chose to waste his wages, it was his responsibility and his alone. If he chose to provide decent shelter, food, clothing, and medical care, etc., for himself and his dependents, it was his responsibility and his alone. That is the picture of paid labor that was painted for all to see. But the reality of this system was an entirely different thing because businessmen were intent on grossly underpaying the workers. As such, the worker would not be able to afford a decent standard of living or capable of making the financial choices that needed to be made. This system of paid labor proclaimed a noble objective, but was actually fueled by a sinister one. "Paid labor," then, was a phrase somewhat akin to a code word; its effect, and probably its intent, was to switch laborers from a system of slavery that they were familiar with, could be critical of and were able to attack to a system of slavery that they did not understand well enough to evaluate critically or fight against effectively.

III. Money Crops, Money Products And Money Services

Money crops, money products and money services were what businessmen in the American colonies wished for day and night. Something a lot of consumers were willing to pay money for on a regular basis, or something that a few consumers were willing to pay a lot of money for occasionally; that was the second key to generating a clear and substantial profit. Such profits could in turn be used to upgrade the businessman's standard of living, project a desired lifestyle or invest in additional commercial activities. They could also fill the coffers of local, state and federal governments and enable them to attract other business interested persons and their money making potential.

In the South, the focus was on crops. Indigo, rice, tobacco and, later, cotton are a few of the crops that turned the South into an agricultural industrial complex. Prior to the Revolutionary War, tobacco led the way. Tobacco destroyed the land's fertility and was wasteful to produce, but it was the agricultural focus of the South nonetheless. Tobacco would be processed into snuff and pipe tobacco and shipped to all parts of Europe because the demand for it was great and Europeans were willing to pay whatever the planters charged. The actual wealth generated in the South by tobacco in the years leading up to the Revolutionary War was astounding, and its potential was such that even a small percentage of the returns equated to a pretty substantial sum of money. Add in the returns from other money crops, and we get a clearer picture of the economic considerations that nourished and generated the split between businessmen in the mother country and businessmen in the colonies.

In the Middle and Northern colonies, fishing, shipbuilding, fur trading and manufacturing industries evolved. However, the money product in New England, beyond question, was liquor. Untold numbers of ships loaded with liquor would leave New England and unload in Europe, take the short trip from Europe to Africa and load up on slaves, unload the slaves in the Caribbean and load up on molasses, and take the molasses from the Caribbean back to New England, where it was used to make more liquor. The production of the next load of liquor would start the process all over again. Needless to say, any disagreement that threatened the profits generated by this activity could have led to a split between the mother country and the colonies.

The industries generated by the money crops of the South and the liquor and manufacturing industries of New England translated into riches throughout the colonies. That is true because many of the support commodities, raw materials and services these industries needed to thrive were provided by the other colonies. Thus, tobacco production was not only critical to the economy of the South, it helped sustain those of the North and West also. The same was true of the liquor industry. In fact, every successful commercial activity depends on and often generates other commercial activities that transcend sectional boundaries. This was just as true in the British colonies as anywhere else.

The money services that were so important to the development of the colonies were most firmly entrenched in New York. During the years leading up to the Revolutionary War, New York had become the investment capital of the colonies, and was on its way to becoming the investment capital of the world. A brief paragraph about the settling of New York will help us understand how this came about.

New York was not like the other American colonies. To begin with, New York (New Amsterdam) was an established Dutch colony, not an English one. The Dutch loved money more than anything else, and they did not try to hide this fact. Religion meant less than money to the Dutch, and they did not deny it. Morality meant less than money to the Dutch, and they did not deny it. Love and humanity meant less than money to the Dutch, and they did not deny it. As such, the commercial development of the colony of New York was not hampered by any of the rationalizations or hypocrisies that fettered the English colonies. The Dutch were primarily interested in making a buck, they did not deny that they were primarily interested in making a buck, and they spent much of their time and energy devising financial schemes and business structures that would make a buck.

Earlier I made the statement that the English were the leading capitalist nation among major European countries. If I had included all European countries, the Dutch would have been given that distinction. Dutch businessmen took money-making ideas like banking, insurance and corporate financing to new heights (and lows), and made dastardly practices like stock exchange manipulation, mindless speculation and investor misinformation basic ingredients of the business experience. To Dutch businessmen, every circumstance was a good or bad financial opportunity. Individuals who were willing to take on the risk and disregard non-business factors could make money under almost any circumstances if they applied the correct business principles. That is what the Dutch believed, that is what they practiced and that is what the colony of New York (New Amsterdam) was built on.

Because of its totally business character, its business at the expense of everything else demeanor, New Amsterdam had become a financially prosperous colony as early as 1650. Individuals in search of money making opportunities flocked there. Most of them failed miserably, so poverty was just as rampant in New Amsterdam as the other colonies; but the ones who succeeded drew the attention of business minded persons and gave New Amsterdam its claim to prosperity. Governments throughout Europe also took note of New Amsterdam's prosperity. Great Britain went a step further. Great Britain declared war on Holland, took New Amsterdam from the Dutch in 1664 and renamed it New York.

From that time on, English settlers flocked to New York. English values merged with Dutch ones and New York became the center of American capitalism. Less than a quarter of a century later, the seeds of Wall Street were bearing fruit and slaves had become the first commodity regularly traded there. Not surprisingly, the colony continued to flourish economically, so much so that by the eve of the American Revolution, the financial leaders of New York were not averse to doing to the British what the British had done to the Dutch 100 years earlier. The only question in their minds was, "Is an American revolution good for business?"

IV. Efficiency Of Operations

When it comes to the issue of economics and finances, the white world has rarely, if ever, been efficient. White economics has specialized in waste more than anything else, and this is borne out clearly in the American colonies. If it had not been for their greed and lack of balance, the businessmen in Europe and the colonies could have recognized the myriad advantages of co-existing with the native Americans, preserving the fertility of America's land, giving people a "fair shake" for their labor, truthfully informing people about investment opportunities and eschewing products that were detrimental to America's health and social fabric. But that required too much long term planning and too many short term sacrifices. In the developing colonial economic scheme, efficiency was simply a code word for profits. Anything beyond profits, no matter how important it might have been, was a negligible economic factor.

What, then, do we find at the core of America's prosperity in the mid-1700s? We find unpaid and underpaid labor. We find a money crop, tobacco, that is socially demeaning and bears no redeeming value, and a money product, liquor, that is just as socially demeaning and unredeeming. And we find the emergence of a "business at all costs" economic demeanor. Is it any wonder, then, that if we fast forward to the year 1900, we find pretty much the same thing? And the year 2000? If we fast forward to the year 2000, it is clear that underpaid labor continues to be a hallmark of American economics. It is also clear that companies like Philip Morris and RJ Reynolds bathe in dollars earned by a product that kills and undermines the health of human beings. It is just as clear that the most glamorous and beloved American families, the Kennedys for example, make their fortunes in the misery that products like liquor produce. And Michael Milken and his ilk? Weren't they predictable? Wasn't corporate America predictable? Yes, and yes again. Why? Because underpaid labor, liquor and tobacco and the like, financial scams, ripping off the public and disregarding the rights of everyday people are not regrettable flukes in the American economic experience, they are critical parts of its essence. Capital centric economics is at the political core of white America, and "political capitalism" is a term that accurately describes its form of government.

CHAPTER FOURTEEN:
THE REVOLUTIONARY WAR PERIOD
(1750 - 1783)

I. Colonial Discontentment

After the settlement of Jamestown, the colonists struggled but gradually became stable. From that point until the early 1700s, the colonists struggled to find a reliable economic base; that is, a product or service they could depend on for a comfortable and stable way of life. During these periods, the colonists frequently felt discontentment toward Great Britain, the mother country. As the years passed, the level of discontentment with Great Britain increased, but the reason for the discontentment took on a different hue. Initially, the colonists were discontented because they felt the mother country was efficient at asserting its authority but reluctant to act in a manner that would ease the economic and security hardships the colonists were experiencing. This type of discontentment, which was in fact a plea for assistance and inclusion, could not have resulted in a serious break with British authority. Later, when the colonists recognized that they could independently satisfy their economic and security needs, the discontentment brought on by British authority was due to the colonists' disinclination to share the wealth they were generating with the British. The expression of this type of discontentment was a horse of a different color. It was a warning, not a plea. It was a declaration of greed. It was a notice to the British that they should watch their step, that the American colonists were being motivated by the money factor and, therefore, would forcefully resist any British efforts to bully them around.

The colonists in the various colonies were drawn closer and closer together each time the British insisted on forcing the colonists to toe the British line. While this reenforced and augmented the colonial impression of Great Britain as an aggressor, it also made the colonies more and more aware of their own differences and heightened their distaste for each other. Thus, even though the United States of America had not been born, the seeds for the War Between the States were already bearing fruit. Since the morality of slavery was not seriously discussed in pre-Revolutionary War America, "freeing the slaves" had little or nothing to do with this developing schism. But let's not get ahead of ourselves. Suffice it to say that, by the mid-1700s, the American colonies were Great Britain's richest possession. An ongoing battle over the profits was a certainty. What was uncertain was how the first stage of this battle would be played out.

II. Pontiac's War

In 1763, Pontiac, chief of the Ottawa, declared war on the English and tried to drive all of the settlers out of the Ohio Valley region. Whites call Pontiac's War a conspiracy, which insinuates that the whites were the good guys and the native Americans were troublemakers. In any event, during Pontiac's siege of Detroit, the French double crossed him by withdrawing their military support at a critical juncture. Pontiac could not make the necessary adjustments and was soon defeated.

Although he was defeated, Pontiac made the British aware of two things. The first was the need to temporarily defuse the resentment for whites felt by Native Americans. With that in mind, the British issued a proclamation that forbade the westward expansion of the whites. No new settlers could occupy land west of the Allegheny Mountains, and all whites who already occupied the restricted area had to withdraw. This made the colonists irate because expanding westward was the key to a myriad of economic opportunities. Fur traders, land speculators, Southern planters and new settlers were counting on the riches offered by westward expansion. Thus, the British proclamation generated colonial resentment because it put an end to a lot of their economic dreams, plans and aspirations.

The second thing Pontiac's War made the British aware of was the fact that a greater British military presence in the colonies was necessary if they were going to adequately protect their investment and maintain order. The colonists interpreted a greater British military presence as a step in the wrong political direction, one that would reduce their rights as Englishmen and render them more vulnerable to British aggression and tyranny. In fact, the American colonists had always enjoyed a relatively high level of self-government. Most colonies were strictly governed by the mother country, but the British did not interfere with the colonial governments in America that much, and the colonists had begun to take that for granted. Additionally, the American colonists had become accustomed to paying less than their fair share of the British tax burden. With the issuance of the aforementioned proclamations, the colonists felt that an unacceptable change was on the way. Their response was to resist.

The British response to the American resistance was to attempt to tighten the reins. The British were serious about getting their fair share of America's profits, so they began enforcing existing trade laws more stringently (the Molasses Act, for example) and issuing new laws that increased the colonial tax burden. The Sugar Act (1764), the Currency Act (1764), the Stamp Act (1765) and the Quartering Act (1765) required the colonists to pay more and more direct and indirect taxes, but the response of the colonists was more and more unequivocal. They refused to use the products that were newly taxed, organized public demonstrations, destroyed stamps and had stamp collectors running out of town to save their lives. The colonists went so far as to say that the British had no right to tax them. After much contention, the British repealed the Stamp Act and loosened the reins a bit (particularly in regards to the Molasses Act). Did they do so because they realized the colonists were right? Not in the least. They did so because the colonial boycott of taxable items was so effective that it was causing the British government to lose an appreciable amount of revenue. Loosening the reins a bit could put an end to those losses.

The fact that the British treasury was nearly dry insured that Parliament would not allow the reins to remain loose for long. In 1767, a Duty Act imposed additional taxes on items such as glass, paper, lead and tea. In response to this, the Massachusetts legislature called for united resistance against Great Britain. In response to the Massachusetts action, the British Parliament dissolved the Massachusetts legislature for issuing the call and the Virginia House of Burgesses for supporting it.

Tensions continued to mount. In 1770, the so-called Boston Massacre took place. In 1773, the Boston Tea Party dumped the tea of a British company into the Boston Harbor. Parliament responded by issuing the so-called Intolerable Acts, which were intended to punish Massachusetts, especially Boston, for resisting British authority. In turn, the colonies formed the First Continental Congress. Since a continental congress is a provisional government, its formation was, in fact, a declaration of the colonies' willingness to split with Great Britain. However, most of the members of the First Continental Congress were conservatives, so they sought a peaceful resolution to the evolving crisis. A review of their demands reveals that they wanted all of the rights and privileges of Englishmen in Great Britain, but they did not want to bear the same economic and political obligations that Englishmen in Great Britain bore.

III. Sectional Incompatibilities

If what has been recorded is true, many settlers felt that if it were not for British authority, which imposed union within the colonies, the colonies would have constantly been in conflict with each other. That is because the colonists, North, South and West, did not like each other, did not trust each other. Long before there was any rippling of revolutionary sentiment, different sectional insecurities and preferences had led to mutual distastes and mutual abhorrence. For example, Southerners were turned off by the self-righteous and holier than thou demeanor of New England Puritans. New Englanders, on the other hand, were critical of the hypocritical posture of "Southern gentlemen." New Yorkers were opposed to anything that interfered with the free flow of business, and they saw a lot to upset them in the religious hypocrisy of New Englanders and the aristocratic posture of Southerners. There were also arguments over ownership and disposition of unsettled territories, currencies, local practices and regulations and external political allegiances. These are the type of differences that intelligent people are able to limit and keep within perspective. But without the imposition of British authority, these differences would have kept the colonies from uniting into what was to become the United States of America.

Even on the eve of the Revolutionary War, the colonists had doubts about independence, and many of these doubts hinged on their distaste for each other. People throughout the colonies looked at Boston, which was the center of anti-British activities, and concluded that economic considerations were at the root of Boston's dissatisfaction with British authority. They felt that slogans like "taxation without representation" and complaints about a standing army were too weak to bear their own weight and were meant to bring the other colonies into a disagreement that they had little or nothing to gain from. Furthermore, many colonists felt that, once Great Britain had been removed, New Englanders would try to run the colonies and mold all of the colonies in New England's image. That, in their opinion, would be worse than British tyranny.

But the disagreement that would have done more than anything else to keep the colonies from uniting revolved around the issue of labor. Southern businessmen would never have willingly formed a union with Northern businessmen because they could not trust Northerners to respect their system of labor, and the same can be said of Northern businessmen in regard to Southerners. The fact that Northern businessmen were right is a worthless point; Southern businessman were either unable to see the advantages of underpaid labor or unable to separate a good idea from a bad source because they abhorred and distrusted that source so completely. After all was said and done, the businessmen knew that, economically speaking, what was good for one section was bad for the other. Labor highlighted the differences, but did not exhaust them. Trade bills that would be good for one section would be terrible for the other, westward expansion on terms that would benefit one section would hamper another, and property rights that were deemed appropriate in one section would be offensive to another. There were too many unpaved roads between Northerners, Westerners and Southerners, and practically all of them led to sectional distrust and incompatibility.

But there was one road all businessmen were familiar with--- maximizing profits. In each section, businessmen recognized that the less money they had to pay the British in taxes, tariffs and duties, etc., the more they could keep for their own pleasure and investments. They also recognized that they could legislate to their advantage if they were not hampered by political forces that were making laws based on other considerations. To them, a revolutionary war could prove to be advantageous, but if one should come about, it would be a consequence of an alliance of convenience between the sections. Once freedom from England had been achieved, each section would be its own master, and neither section would be hampered by another one. It is with this thought in mind that the unity of the colonies rested on the eve of the American Revolutionary War. It would prove to be a capable foundation.

CHAPTER FIFTEEN:
THE REVOLUTIONARY WAR

I. The Business of War

Business defines the United States of America. The original settlements were business ventures with typical business objectives, concerns and decisions. But a colonial settlement is not as limited a business as a store. Whereas a store owner hires employees and pays them to take on the duties and seek the objectives of the store owner, a colonial settlement involves a huge number of people who take on a huge number of interests and objectives that go beyond those of the original business. It is this huge number of people and their diverse interests and objectives that caused a distinct American identity to evolve, and resulted in a war for independence.

The initial American settlements were English businesses run by English businessmen. By the eve of the American Revolution, the American colonies had evolved into decentralized American businesses and institutions run by independent American businessmen according to formal and informal guidelines established by regional political figures and customs. These businessmen and political figures were fish of different sizes who influenced ponds of different dimensions. The smallest fish were renown and influential on a local level, but little known and relatively lacking in influence beyond local boundaries. Larger fish were renown and influential on the county level, but little known and relatively lacking in influence beyond the county. Still others had reputations, power and influence that extended throughout a colony and, rather infrequently, throughout all of the colonies. These various levels of financial and political influence were responsible for many of the images projected to most settlers during the period leading up to the Revolutionary War.

Where the individuals of influence throughout the colonies stood on independence was generally determined

by economic considerations. Those who felt their financial interests would be best served by maintaining the
status quo were against the war and often did what they
could to thwart the colonial war effort. On the other hand,
those who felt they could improve their financial lot if
the colonies became independent supported the colonial
war effort. There were, as is always the case, "other considerations," but none of these "other considerations,"
individually or collectively, were capable of generating
the levels of energy needed to spawn war type activities.
Only economic concerns could do that. This was particularly the case among that ilk of self-serving and ego-
centric colonials who thought they were a cut above the
everyday man and woman.

II. The Burden of War

A revolutionary war would affect the day to day activities of all of the colonists, but the condition of most
of the colonists would not be affected at all by the outcome of such a war. The everyday colonist was well aware
of this. If the British won, most of the colonists would
continue to live a life of relative mediocrity. If the colonials
won, most of the colonists would continue to live a life of
relative mediocrity. In New England, they would continue
to work on their small farms and in their small shops, eke
out a living in a variety of other menial and disgusting
ways, pray in their small churches, wear the barest of
clothes, eat the slightest of meals, sleep in drafty lean-
tos and log cabins, identify with the white elites, dehumanize all people of color and acknowledge the right of
white people to rob Black men, women and children of
the fruits of their labor. In the middle colonies, they would
continue to work on their small farms and in their small
shops, eke out a living in a variety of other menial and
disgusting ways, pray in their small churches, wear the
barest of clothes, eat the slightest of meals, sleep in
drafty lean-tos and log cabins, identify with the white
elites, dehumanize all people of color and acknowledge

the right of white people to rob Black men, women and children of the fruits of their labor. And in the South, the everyday colonists would continue to work their small plots of land, eke out a living in a variety of other menial and disgusting ways, pray in their small churches, wear the barest of clothes, eat the slightest of meals, sleep in drafty lean-tos and log cabins, dehumanize all people of color and acknowledge the right of white people to rob Black men, women and children of the fruits of their labor. The war would not improve their standard of living, enable them to patch their leaking roof or drafty cabin, add some needed pieces to their wardrobe, reduce the nature of their debts, increase the size of their congregation or change their attitude about anything of significance. Indeed, the war was not the business of the everyday man and woman, and only involved them because the elites had everything to gain or lose from their participation.

Governments, businesses and business persons rarely put their lives on the line when they have little or nothing to gain or lose. Why, then, do everyday people who have nothing to gain or lose fight in a war? That would be the million dollar question if it were not answered so often. At one turn, they fight because they identify with and are influenced by the propaganda of the elites in their locality. At another turn, they fight because they believe in the propaganda of patriotism more than the individuals and governments that generate that propaganda. At a third turn, they fight because they are more idealistic and less self-centered than the elites. Individuals who have little or nothing to gain or lose also fight because they are convinced they will be punished if they don't fight. And, all too often, they fight because they expect to be paid. Yes, for far too many individuals, the only opportunity they get to work and receive a paycheck on a regular basis is during a war. This was certainly the case in the American colonies on the eve of the Revolutionary War period.

Because of all of the above reasons, the everyday

man and woman in the American colonies would bear the burden of the Revolutionary War. While most of those who would benefit from the war held meetings in obscure buildings in obscure towns and debated obscure issues, everyday people met on the battlefields, where they terrorized, bludgeoned, maimed and killed each other. They marched countless miles, exposed themselves to the harsh elements on countless days and nights, heard cannons and guns explode on countless occasions, felt their flesh rip and blood rush out during countless battles-- and were left to face the wrath of the enemy alone when they suffered a countless number of ill-timed injuries. They left parents, spouses, siblings and offspring alone and unprotected during the most dangerous of times; left them to shed tears that should not have been shed, suffer levels of privation that should not have been suffered, and endure life draining degrees of stress that should never have been endured. And, after all was said and done, after the war had been fought and insanely reached its end, those who had not been killed returned to the same inadequate plot of land, the same inadequate food, clothing and shelter, the same unjust system of indebtedness, the same mediocrity and the same utterly hopeless existence that they had left at the beginning of the war. But it was not all for nought, their elites assured them, because a new, better nation had emerged. The everyday white American man and woman should rejoice, their elites assured them, because they were no longer at the beck and call of the British king or unjust British rule. That was true. They were no longer at the beck and call of the British king, but they were at the beck and call of an American elite. Should they rejoice, or was it all for nought indeed?

It was called the American Revolutionary War, but it was not a revolution at all. At best, it was an offshore coup d'etat, a long distance shake up of the political status quo. At worst, it was a bloody way to close the books on a business transaction gone bad.

III. That's Why They Fight The War

On paper, there was no way the American colonies could win a war against Great Britain. The British army was the most powerful in the world, led by the best trained military leaders of the time. The British army, which was made up of experienced fighters, had left their mark throughout the world as they converted a small English nation into the huge British Empire. The British navy was the mistress of the seas, and struck fear in opponents that were much better able to defend themselves than the American colonies. And the British government was one of the most organized and best connected in the world. Of all of the countries of contemporary Europe, the British were the best at devising a series of strategic activities and raising the money needed to finance those activities. Great Britain was the Goliath of contemporary Europe; a Goliath with brains, experience, technological superiority and wherewithal. The American colonies, on the other hand, were David without a slingshot. On paper, the American colonies did not stand the slightest chance of emerging victorious.

Additionally, there was a great deal of support for Great Britain in the colonies. Some colonists were close to the English crown, and many, like the Quakers in Pennsylvania and Delaware, were advocates of peace. Meanwhile, many of the individuals who played major roles in the colonial effort were more concerned about their personal cause than any other. As a result, John Hancock, the president of the First Continental Congress, wavered back and forth, sometimes siding with the rebellers, sometimes leaning toward selling out to the British. Dr Benjamin Church, another member of the Continental Congress, was an outright traitor; one on a long list of prominent American "heros" who were actually passing on vital information at vital times to the British. But we must remember: traitors and scoundrels are part and parcel of every nationalistic movement. The war for American independence, and countless other conflicts, are proof that success can be had in spite of them.

The following is an understatement: the American colonies were not prepared to fight a war. To begin with, they had no ammunition. Nor did they have an ammunition source; a business or government they could rely on to supply them with ammunition. In the colonies, from the very beginning, all able-bodied men had been required to bear arms. This helped when hostilities broke out, but the men in the colonies did not maintain arsenals or produce ammunition in quantities that were needed to conduct and sustain a war. A war is a group effort, not an individual one; it is a concerted process. Individuals who own guns do not an army make.

In addition to not having ammunition, the colonies had no support infrastructure. They had no one to supply them with the non-fighting materials needed to conduct a war, nor anyone to co-ordinate such an effort. They had no source of clothing or uniforms, no food supply, no blankets, no mules and horses, no means of transportation, no organized means of communication. If the native Americans had been sufficiently organized, and if the British were to not interfere, it is doubtful that the colonies could have defeated the original occupants of the land so convincingly. In that regard, it was ludicrous to think they could defeat the British.

But even worse, the colonies had no army and no worthwhile military experience. George Washington, the man who was named General of the Colonial Army, had never played a prominent role in any successful military engagement. Worse still, in those where he played a major role, it would be an understatement to say that he had failed. The term failure does not begin to describe how pitifully he had represented himself, how utterly incapable he had proven to be. In a military sense, George Washington was so stupid that he built a fort at the foot of a hill during the French and Indian War; AT THE FOOT OF A HILL! How could he be expected to lead a rebellious collection of colonies to victory?

The colonies did not know, in concrete terms, what their relationship was to each other. How, then, could they efficiently conduct a revolutionary war? The answer is simple: THEY COULDN'T!

If their choice had been strictly a logical one, the colonists never would have moved in the direction of war. But historical developments are much more than paper predictions, much more than research, analysis and logical conclusions. History is the harnessing and release of varying degrees of energy, and logic is not the only powerful factor that needs to be taken into account. Myriads of beliefs, emotions, misfortunes and indiscretions come together and remind logic of its limitations. Factors that are entirely alien to the issue at hand intercede as well, forcing a redeployment of resources, obscuring the time line and changing the relative value of relied upon assets and liabilities. Before one realizes it, the issue begins playing out in a way that is much different from what the paper had anticipated. That is why winners insist on resolving the issue that way. As they say in sports, "that is why they play the game." And in politics, that is why they fight the war.

IV. They Fight The War

From 1776 until 1783 they fought the war. The American forces, incompetent and disorganized at the top, overly composed of undisciplined individuals who resented authority at the bottom, and suffering from every imaginable privation throughout, were incapable of winning the war. However, the British were quite capable of losing it, and that is exactly what took place.

As was stated earlier, on paper everything was in Britain's favor. However, what was on paper represented Britain during the best of times. Serious students of history come to realize that a small social or political shift here or there can translate into big but relatively imperceptible changes, changes that frequently escape the notice of paper brokers. Under stressful conditions, these changes, totally unexpected, confront the favored party with unanticipated snags and obstacles, call for adjustments that frustrate and fluster a complex structure and present the underdog with favorable and inspirational opportunities. Such was the case during the Revolutionary War. Britain, coming off of the war with France, was unable or unwilling to generate the energy needed to conduct another war. This lack of energy was evident in all aspects of Britain's wartime performance. Britain's financial movers and shakers, lacking the necessary urgency and fervor, failed to raise enough money to bankroll the war. Money was raised, but it was a very difficult sell; it required much too much energy per dollar. Britain's well trained and experienced army was now war weary, and recruiting capable men who were willing to travel 3000 miles to fight required more energy than British recruiters could muster. As a result, too many of the men who enlisted were not good soldiers, and were prone to panic and be disorderly. Additionally, Britain's propaganda machine sputtered, while those who sympathized with the Americans eagerly expended huge quantities of energy to make the war unpopular in Britain. On top of all of this were the puzzling conduct of Britain's military leaders and the sudden inappropriateness of the British political system. Those in control of the military effort made blunders that only divided allegiances and disinterested parties could make, while those in control of the diplomatic effort failed to realize that the American establishment was opposed to fighting a war against Great Britain. The American leaders gave the British every opportunity to appease them and maintain the status quo because they were accustomed to and comfortable with British rule. By contrast, an independent America might allow poor people that American leaders despised and mistrusted to play too prominent a role in the political process. America's leadership, for the most part, was as anti-revolution as Great Britain's leadership, but Great Britain was unable to perceive that huge advantage and benefit from it.

The lethargic British response and the resolve of the colonists to fight in spite of the odds and see the war through convinced the French that outright support of the Americans was worth the risk. Under ideal circumstances, even if their sympathies had been pro-American, the French would not have taken so bold and defiant a step against Great Britain, but the more the colonists fought the war, the more everyone realized that the actual war would be quite different from the war the paper brokers had anticipated. In fact, what was actually achievable was so different from what everyone believed that support for the Americans became more than a part of France's political scheme to undo Great Britain, it became a French cause celebre.

Thus, a rebellion of unorganized farmers that would have been quickly squashed under ideal conditions managed to mosey on along, establish a little bit of momentum and sustain itself. After that, even though they might not have realized it at the time, the key was not to defeat the British, but to hang on long enough for Great Britain to crumble under the weight of its own inertia. Each succeeding political and military blunder increased the dead weight the British had to carry more than it should have, and increased the confidence of the American farmers and their allies more than it should have. As has occurred so often in history, the impossible was happening. David was slinging shots that should not have deterred Goliath in the least. But, lo and behold, Goliath was not only acting disoriented, Goliath was stumbling and falling to the ground.

The American rebels could not have defeated the British, but they did not have to. What they had to do was (1) demonstrate a willingness to fight for what they believed in (2) fight as bravely, effectively and efficiently as they could (3) persevere and refuse to give in (4) represent themselves as a serious member of the international family of nations and (5) resolve to accept the outcome of their efforts, be they favorable or not so favorable. No, the Americans could not have defeated the British, but if they had not taken themselves seriously, they would not have been able to take advantage of Britain's ability to defeat itself. The Americans took on the challenge! They fought against what they thought were overwhelming odds, and they have to be given credit for that. They convinced themselves that only liberty and death were acceptable, and they must be commended for having the nerve. Even though they were poorly organized, they took their diplomatic case to the world with the same degree of pride and assurance that the British, French and Spanish would have displayed. No, the Americans did not defeat the British, but they placed their destiny into their own hands, took on the responsibilities winners take on and emerged victorious. They could not have done anything more.

V. Victory

The first battle of the war, between the towns of Lexington and Concord in Massachusetts, established a British pattern of ineptness and augured the British fate. Because of bad military decisions, the British would find themselves in an untenable position, but were still superior enough to defeat the settlers in face to face combat. However, when the settlers were smart enough to hit and run, the British did not have enough composure to maintain rank and fully exploit their advantage. As a result, when the British emerged victorious, it would often be a tainted victory that not only deflated the British, but inspired the colonials. Over a period of time, the effect mushroomed and ballooned to the extent that the British, with superior forces, were fighting with the mindset of losers, while the settlers, with inferior forces, were fighting with the mindset of winners.

In spite of Britain's ineptness, the British would have won the war had it not been for Benedict Arnold. Benedict Arnold, the one military leader the British learned to respect, and the one colonial whose military daring filled the British with awe and fear, provided the Americans with an inspirational military performance time and time again. While George Washington did not know how to function pro-actively, Benedict Arnold took the offensive and forced the British to make decisions they might not have otherwise been ready to make. Before the 2nd Continental Congress convened, Arnold teamed with Ethan Allan and took Fort Ticonderoga and, in 1777, defeated the British at Saratoga in the Battle that convinced the French to support the American cause. Later, Arnold decided that serving the British would be more personally rewarding, so he turned traitor. If he had not done so, he might have become president of the United States after the war ended.

By the time of Arnold's betrayal, the Americans had begun to believe they could emerge victorious. They persevered and, in the process, allowed the British the time they needed to self destruct. As the war in America revealed more and more of Britain's weaknesses, more and more of Britain enemies in Europe launched attacks against her. By 1782, Great Britain was eager to end the war in America in order to better fight against her European enemies. As a result, in 1783 the Treaty of Paris ended the American Revolutionary War, and the American colonies became free and independent states.

CHAPTER SIXTEEN:
THE ARTICLES OF CONFEDERATION (1781 - 1787)

I. Establishing A Provisional Government

In response to measures like the Stamp Act, the Molasses Act, the Boston Massacre and the blockading of Boston's port, the settlers in the various colonies began to unite in order to more effectively resist the British. This united resistance culminated in the establishment of the First Continental Congress on September 5, 1774.

A continental congress is a temporary, provisional government. People form temporary, provisional governments when they realize that the established government needs to be re-made or replaced. The established government in the colonies represented the interests of the British crown and Parliament. What the settlers needed was a government that would represent their interests. They formed this government and called it the First Continental Congress.

The First Continental Congress was an illegal government because it did not meet the approval of the British Parliament, so its members were in danger of being arrested by British authorities and military people. In the eyes of the British government, the colonies broke the law when they called for and formed the First Continental Congress. However, the First Continental Congress was not illegal in the eyes of the American colonists. To them, it was a meeting of 55 men from various colonies whose mission was to discuss the issues that most affected the colonies. The delegates to the First Continental Congress did not have any authority, and only two colonies, Maryland and North Carolina, were serious enough to declare that they would stand behind the decisions made by the Congress. This lack of esteem accorded to a temporary, provisional government during its early stages is par for the nationalist course, as is witnessed in the year 2000 by the lack of attention Black

People pay to the Provisional Government of the Republic of New Afrika. Esteem and importance, however, are entirely different realities. As lightly esteemed as it was at the time, the First Continental Congress was of paramount importance because it represented the beginning of self-government for the American colonies.

The delegates to the First Continental Congress wanted all of the advantages of being a British citizen but few of the responsibilities. They wanted to govern themselves, but they did not want to separate from Great Britain. While they were trying to figure out how to walk that tightrope, local assemblymen in Massachusetts were forming their own free state, urging the people to arm themselves and calling for economic boycotts of all English products and services. Faced with such decisive independent actions, the delegates to the First Continental Congress had no choice but to support the Massachusetts assembly. Even though they did not want to, the delegates issued a Declaration of Rights of the American colonies, outlined a number of British abuses and adopted agreements stating that none of the colonies would import products from Great Britain, export products to Great Britain or consume any British products. On October 22, 1774, less than seven weeks after arriving in Philadelphia, the First Continental Congress agreed to meet again in May, 1775.

On May 10, 1775, the Second Continental Congress met in Philadelphia. During the seven month period since the First Continental Congress had adjourned, Massachusetts had virtually declared its independence. The province of Massachusetts had elected its own president, appointed a treasurer to collect taxes and commissioned a committee of safety to collect arms and ammunition, organize the minute men, set up a system of intelligence to spy on the British and set up a line of military defense in case the British should attack. Additionally, the governor of Virginia had issued land grants in the West that were in complete defiance of the British policy on Western lands, and had authorized and implemented a war against the native Americans who occupied those lands. And, most importantly, only three weeks earlier, the British army had clashed with colonists at Concord, Massachusetts, killing a handful of them. However, by the time the British soldiers were able to return to safety, their ranks had been devastated by colonial guerillas and minute men. The weaknesses of the British army had been exposed for all to see.

After opening, the Second Continental Congress became aware of something else: Ethan Allen and his Green Mountain Boys had taken Fort Ticonderoga from the British. In spite of not wanting to take bold actions, the members of the Second Continental Congress knew that their hands were forced. Consequently, the Second Continental Congress declared that it had power over "Indian" relations, declared that the military actions of the people in Massachusetts were actions of the Army of the United Colonies, appointed George Washington as the Commander in Chief of the Army, considered establishing a 14th colony for Native Americans, authorized an expedition into Canada for the purpose of making Canada the 14th colony and authorized other acts of war. Still, the Second Continental Congress did not call for independence. That, for the most part, is due to the fact that members of the Continental Congress were more comfortable with the tyranny of British elites than the involvement of the masses that American independence would necessitate.

The actions of the Second Continental Congress fell far short of what John Adams called for. Adams' program called for the seizure of all British officials, the institution of a government in each colony, a declaration of freedom for the colonies and the resumption of harmonious relations between Great Britain and the new American country. But developments were taking place throughout the colonies that sped the colonies toward independence, and forced the hand of the delegates to the Second Continental Congress. In December of 1775, some colonial patriots burned the city of Norfolk, but convinced the public that the British had done so. Virginia, which had been a leading proponent of independence, was now more convinced than ever. Also, local patriots in the Carolinas had attacked and driven off a British fleet, which left the Carolinas no choice but to seek independence. Add to this the facts that a small fleet of continental ships had seized control of Nassau and Washington had moved into Boston, forcing the British to flee, and it is clear that the Second Continental Congress had to vote for independence. This took place in July of 1776.

While the Revolutionary War dragged along, the Second Continental Congress, an illegal, temporary, provisional government that was always "on the run" (they were always running from the British soldiers that had orders to arrest them), feeblemindedly and haphazardly governed the colonies. As events proved, this feebleminded and haphazard government served the purpose until March 1, 1781, when the Articles of Confederation were adopted. With the adoption of the Articles of Confederation, a new country, the United States of America, was officially formed and, based on all outward appearances, a perpetual United States government installed.

II. The Articles of Confederation

The Articles of Confederation, the first constitution of the United States of America, was proposed on June 11, 1776, agreed upon by Congress 18 months later on November 15, 1777 and ratified on March 1, 1781. The Articles of Confederation was a states rights document; it recognized the supremacy of each state as an independent political entity. Federally, the Articles of Confederation revolved around a Congress that was supposed to govern the country (Congress was not supposed to govern each state). Since Congress was not in session year round, a committee composed of one representative from each state was selected to run the country in Congress' absence. Out of this committee, one person who actually ran the country was chosen as president. John Hanson, a major player in the Revolution and an extremely influential member of Congress, was the first person chosen to run the country when Congress was not sitting and, therefore, became the country's first President.

As the first president, Hanson had to blaze an unexplored trail. The role of president was not clearly defined, so no one knew in specific terms what the president should do. As a result, Hanson's actions in office would set precedents for all future presidents. He assumed his duties at about the end of the Revolutionary War, when the country was penniless, the federal government was weak and middling and the troops who had fought for independence wanted to be paid. In fact, the troops threatened to use their weapons to overthrow the new government and make George Washington king. While most of the members of Congress responded by running for their lives, Hanson stood his ground, appeased the troops as best he could and kept the new country from splitting up. Thus, acting as the first President of the United States under the Articles of Confederation, John Hanson saved the union, a feat that was not to be matched until Abraham Lincoln did likewise more than 80 years later.

As President, Hanson ordered all foreign troops, British, Spanish and French included, to leave American soil. Hanson also established the Great Seal of the United States, the first Treasury Department, the first Secretary of War, and the first Foreign Affairs Department. In addition to that, Hanson declared that the fourth Thursday of every November would be Thanksgiving Day. Needless to say, John Hanson's impact on the institutionalizing of this country has been nothing less than noteworthy.

The Articles of Confederation only permitted a person to serve a single one-year term as president in any three-year period, so Hanson's term ended on November 3, 1782. Six other presidents were elected to one year terms after John Hanson, but students of white American history learn little or nothing about them. Why is this the case? An understanding of the Articles of Confederation and the America that existed under the Articles will reveal the answer to that question.

The Articles of Confederation is one of the most carefully thought out documents ever produced by America's founding fathers. It established a "perpetual union" of the states, and the term perpetual is pointedly repeated several times in the document. As was just stated, the Articles made it clear that running the country was the job of Congress (in Congress' absence, a president actually carried out that function). The Articles also named the country the United States of America, called for the annual appointment of delegates, and provided that no person could be a delegate for more than three years in any six year period, nor president for more than one year in any three year period. Under the Articles, no State would have less than two, nor more than seven members in Congress, and when Congress assembled, each State would have one vote.

Like the men who drew up the Constitution a few yeas later, the men who drew up the Articles of Confederation were white businessmen; businessmen from the Southern, Middle and Northern states. But because they were in the midst of the American Revolutionary War and overly sensitive to the potential abuses of big government, they thought their interests would be best served by localizing government to the greatest extent possible. They wanted to make sure that a large American government would not be able to impose its will on the smaller state governments the way Great Britain had imposed its will on the colonies. Their United States of America was viewed as a "friendship" characterized by independent ("strong") state governments and a dependent ("weak") central government.

This preference for localization manifested itself in business terms as well. Because of the fierce independence that characterized businessmen and business procedures up to that point, the producers of the Articles of

Confederation felt that it was to their economic advantage to permit as much leeway as possible for individual businessmen. They felt it would be better for business and more advantageous for businessmen if they were faced with working their way around state and local laws and ordinances rather than national ones. We must remember: the representatives from the various colonies harbored a great deal of dislike and distrust for each other. Much of this dislike was due to tensions generated by the contrasting economic realities that drove the various colonies. Thus, even as they united for political independence, they knew they wanted as little as possible to do with each other after independence had been gained. Therefore, they made sure that the constitution that "unified" them guaranteed the required degree of "independence" for each of them.

III. The Articles of Confederation: Danger Signs

There are several danger alerts that jump out at one who reviews the Articles of Confederation. To begin with, it proposes that a body of men (Congress) run the country. It is very difficult to get a body of men to agree on anything, and when it does come to an agreement, it is rarely in a timely fashion. This noticeably slowed the process of government. But the producers of the Articles of Confederation were well aware of this disadvantage when they included it--- IT WAS MEANT TO BE THAT WAY!! To make sure government didn't slow down too much, the men who produced the Articles included a provision that authorized a single person out of a committee of the states to take on the responsibility of actually running the country during non-emergency times. This person was called the president.

Another danger alert of the Articles is that it did not call for a popularly elected president. Again, the producers of the Articles of Confederation were well aware of this fact--- IT TOO WAS MEANT TO BE THAT WAY!! These men were not thinking about creating a democracy, not even a republic for that matter; they held as much contempt for and fear of the everyday person as did the king of England. Thus, they were completely against the rule of ONE MAN, but they were all for the rule of ONE small, elite GROUP of men. Their mission, then, was to create a government that enabled each state to be ruled by a small group of influential white men. What they created was exactly what they wanted.

A third danger alert was the lack of power granted to the confederation, the central government. For the third time, IT WAS MEANT TO BE THAT WAY!! The producers of the Articles of Confederation knew about the advantages and disadvantages of a strong central government; most of them had done a great deal of research and study in that particular area. Because they understood the issue so well, they were opposed to it, absolutely opposed to it! They knew, without doubt, that they did not want a central government that could impose its will on the state and local governments. Consequently, they formed a government of STATES in "a firm league of friendship with each other." They could have just as easily formed a government that merged the various states into one huge country that was ruled by one huge government. However, one huge government, of necessity, would have to revolve around a political process that was too far from their immediate reaches. They didn't want that, they didn't want anything that even resembled that!

CHAPTER SEVENTEEN:
LIFE UNDER THE ARTICLES OF CONFEDERATION

I. Everyday People and Elites

Under the Articles of Confederation, life for the everyday settlers, now American citizens, was essentially unchanged. They had little to no authority as subjects of the king, and little to no authority as citizens of the newly formed United States of America. Their day-to-day activities, economically, socially, religiously and politically speaking, were not noticeably affected by the change from one man to constitutional rule. That is because what they gained from the Revolutionary War, if the truth be told, was ephemeral and vicarious, not real. The Revolutionary War was not waged to change their lives, it was waged to change the lives of America's upper crust, America's elites. Constitutional government gave the everyday citizen hope that was not present under the king's rule, but it did little to transform that hope into material and concrete realities. Thus, everyday citizens could feel proud that they had fought, acquired their independence and exalt in that glory, but for them, the rewards were essentially idyllic and scarcely concrete. Everyday citizens could revel in the ideology, the euphoria, of this relatively new thing called constitutional government, and they could see how constitutional government had generated concrete, advantageous changes for America's elites, but they could not point to concrete advantages of similar ilk for themselves. Everyday citizens could identify with and boast of their association with and access to the real beneficiaries of the Revolutionary War, but unlike the real beneficiaries, they could not produce anything of concrete value to prove that the war was worth the effort for them. The Articles of Confederation, like the American constitution that usurped it, was not of the people, by the people or for the people. The Articles served the interests of America's elites, and that is exactly what it was intended to do.

Yet, the Articles of Confederation that businessmen and power seekers produced enhanced the political influence of everyday people. The Articles was a states rights document that put power in the hands of the local "elites," but by doing that it put the decision makers closer to everyday political activists and rendered decision makers susceptible to the outbursts and reactions of politically savvy street mobs and gangs. Unfortunately, the Articles of Confederation did not legally empower the masses or grant the masses the authority to make a lawful impact on the political process. That, once again, was by design; the Articles of Confederation was not intended to be a democratic document. Democracy was far from the minds of the leaders of revolutionary America and the creators of the Articles. They wanted a constitution that would address the priorities of business centric politicians in the manner they wanted them addressed. In the Articles, they had exactly that document.

II. Everyday People

In earlier chapters to this book, I talked about "Peers and Peons" and "Education and Miseducation." A review of those chapters will help one understand how everyday people could be both attached to and disconnected from the Articles of Confederation.

Because of the mindset that was brought to the new land from Europe, and because Europe's masses had been schooled to value information that sprung from among Europe's peers and served the interests of Europe's peers, everyday people held the belief that some individuals were better than others and were more entitled to wield power and possess wealth and riches. If members of an elite established a political or economic system, everyday people tended to not challenge the legitimacy of that system. For that reason, they idly accepted the concept of kingship. Even though the concept of kingship would never have originated among everyday people, everyday people were not likely to do anything to de-legitimize the concept or dethrone a king (except in a moment of rage). It is with this kind of disinterested attachment or passive disconnectedness that the average citizen regarded all forms of government, and the Articles of Confederation was no exception.

Since American settlers had fought for a constitutional form of government, they felt better about constitutional rule than one man rule. In spite of that, life for them under the Articles of Confederation was essentially the same as it had been under King George. Thus, they could get along with the Articles of Confederation-- and they could get along without it. The Articles did not present any problems that they were not already accustomed to enduring, and it did not present them with any perks that made it worthy of a vigorous defense. Life was not what everyday citizens wanted it to be under the Articles, but life had never been what everyday citizens wanted it to be.

Because the Articles was a states rights constitution, everyday citizens were closer to the decision making process than they had ever been before. As such, matters tended to be decided in a manner that best benefitted the state, the state's business community and, theoretically at least, the state's inhabitants. It is certain that many everyday citizens were aware of this theoretical advantage. How much they could convert the theory into reality is a matter of uncertainty.

In a word, what everyday citizens felt about the Articles of Confederation was ambivalence. Ambivalence is what most citizens of a nation feel about the government in power. That explains why more citizens tend to ignore political processes and events than participate in them.

III. Elites

Ambivalence is not a sentiment that applies when one summarizes what elite groups feel about a political system. Unlike everyday citizens, elite groups and individuals are constantly trying to make a system serve the purpose of their particular group. As long as they can manipulate the system to serve their needs, elite groups are satisfied with that system. When elite groups can not manipulate a system to serve their ends, they try to destroy that system.

Unlike everyday citizens, the Articles of Confederation had a profound impact on the lives of certain white men; the businessmen and politicians who seized control of the new nation. First and foremost, the power, authority and legitimacy that had once been vested in the king was now vested in their hands and primed to be used to their advantage. They were certain of three things: (1) they wanted no part of one man rule (2) they wanted no part of democratic rule and (3) they did not want influential men from other states meddling in and presiding over the affairs of their state. They had made certain that the constitution they drew up would preclude each of those possibilities.

However, at the time the Articles was created, the scope of their business and political concerns was local and regional, not national. That is why the Articles of Confederation was a states right document. To them, what was good for business could best be promoted by local decision makers, not national ones. To them, local decision makers were better equipped to assess local and regional market conditions and initiate measures that would promote "the general welfare." At the onset, most of America's elites were quite content with the Articles of Confederation.

IV. Seeds of Discontent

As was just stated, at the time of its writing and ratification, the elites were quite satisfied with the Articles of Confederation. However, the prosperous American economy slowed to a crawl when the Revolutionary War ended. Postwar deflation and depression hit the country hard, and the nature of how business was done began to experience some fundamental changes. These changes functioned best within the context of a uniform currency and a strong central government that could raise its own tax revenue and regulate commerce. The Articles of Confederation did not provide for either of these. In fact, in that regard the Articles were built around an opposiing set of political and commercial priorities. Under the Articles, each state was its own empire, issued its own currency, collected its own taxes, and, theoretically, contributed to a common pot that provided the central government with the funds it needed to operate. Additionally, the central government was denied the power to tax. These incompatible priorities developed into hot issues and made people realize that the Articles of Confederation needed to be amended.

The states were not opposed to amending the Articles of Confederation, but the states were opposed to any amendment that would make the state governments subservient to the central government. If the shortcomings of the Articles could have been overcome or appreciably ameliorated by passing amendments that did not change the fundamental relationship between the states and federal governments, the states would probably have agreed to those amendments. But no such amendments were introduced.

If it had been left up to everyday citizens and others who were not intent on having their way, the new American nation would have confronted the future with the Articles of Confederation as its constitution. But there were those who were intent on having things their way. There were those who were determined to make the system serve their purpose-- or destroy it; and they were all motivated by monetary and business considerations. Holders of government securities wanted a federal government that would pay them off on demand. Under the Articles they would be paid, but on the government's schedule, not theirs. They were unwilling to wait. Manufacturers and merchants wanted a government that could establish tariffs that would protect them against foreign competition and squeeze concessions from foreign governments. Under the Articles, this could be done if the states cooperated to a sufficient degree, but business forces were not willing to wait long enough to allow an efficient system of state cooperation to evolve. In their estimation, it would take too much time. Financiers wanted a central government that could control inflation. Concerted actions by independent states, they reasoned, could not do this effectively enough. And real estate speculators wanted a government that could conquer Native Americans ("Indians") in the West, take their land and open it to settlement and financial exploitation. Under the Articles, the individual states could have carried out this function. Speculators reasoned, however, that independent states could not perform that function as consistently and efficiently as a central government. The only solution was to amend the Articles so that the states would be subservient to the central government, or undo the Articles altogether.

On cursory examination, one might be amazed to see all of these different business concerns focussing in on a single culprit and single solution to all of their financial woes. As a serious student would imagine, this was not an impulsive or spontaneous idea that independently jumped into the minds of all of these complainants. There were influences that were common to all of them, and they will be discussed shortly. But first, a critical point must be made clear that has not been given sufficient attention prior to this time. That point is the following: The new nation, the United States of America, could have moved into the future with the Articles of Confederation as its constitution and done quite well!

In 1787, the Articles of Confederation was the most progressive and most business-oriented "law of the land" in the white world. Neither England, Spain, France or any other European nation had a basic law of the land that was as pro-business or politically inclusive as the Articles of Confederation. Additionally, all of Europe's countries were being confronted by the same economic and political realities that were confronting the newly established American nation. They, however, met the future by re-balancing and blending new components into their es-tablished forms of government. America could have done the same and progressed appreciably. Certainly, with a weak central government, the new country would have been less efficient in resisting invasions, but it would have resisted and maintained its sovereignty nonetheless. And the domestic shortcomings that accompany a weak cen-tral government would have had a negative impact, but they would probably have been addressed over an ap-propriate period of time. No, it was not the political sub-servience of the central government that made the Ar-ticles reprehensible in the eyes of America's elites in the late 1780s, it was the central government's economic subservience. Therefore, because of purely economic considerations, the political and social fabric of the en-tire country was plotted against, attacked, sabotaged and usurped.

The United States of America would not have stood still if the Articles of Confederation had remained the law of the land, but it probably would not have grown fast enough financially to satisfy America's business elites. They wanted to fill their pockets, stockpile their accounts and multiply their bottom lines; and they wanted to do them all immediately. With those objectives in mind, and realizing they could not legally amend the Articles, they considered the merits of dissolving the union or hatching a constitutional coup d'etat. They decided on the coup d'etat.

V. The Straws That Stirred The Milkshake

As was stated earlier, there were influences that were common to all of the representatives of business that focussed in on the Articles as the single culprit and single solution to all of their financial woes. Changing the basic law of the land was not an impulsive or spontaneous idea, and it did not independently jump into the minds of such

a wide range of financial complainants. Three developments took place that made business interests dream
about amassing profits that they had never imagined probable before. One was an emerging vision of machine labor (an industrial revolution) that would generate unheard
of profits. The second was the publishing of Adam Smith's
The Wealth of Nations in the United States. The third
was the evolution of Wall Street.

VI. The Industrial Revolution

In the early 1700s, peoples' eyes were being opened
to the possibility of radical changes in the production of
many types of goods and services. People began to realize that, instead of using their hands and simple tools to
do work and produce goods, they could build machines
that would perform the same tasks; more quickly, more
efficiently and in greater volumes. By the late 1700s,
the ideological projections were so astounding and the
pace of innovation so rapid that people's day to day values and activities were being fundamentally altered. This
system, later called the Industrial Revolution, contained
all of its essential features and was firmly in place by
1810.

To understand how the Industrial Revolution impacted
on the business psyche of the United States immediately
after the Revolutionary War, one need only consider the
following facts:

(1) The period when the United States of America
was born and endured its infant years is the very same
period that the industrial revolution was "growing up."
During this same time span, future thinking businessmen
were beginning to realize how much money and commercial activity the Industrial Revolution was capable of generating.

(2) England, the mother country of the United States,
became the home of the Industrial Revolution because it
had what the Industrial Revolution required: markets, capital, labor, raw materials and know-how. Being made in

England's image and possessing all of the requirements just mentioned, the American colonies were, unwittingly, just as capable of nurturing the Industrial Revolution as England.

(3) The first money crop to take advantage of the Industrial Revolution was cotton. In the 1700s, the American colonies were the greatest source of cotton in the world. Even though cotton had not reached its peak in 1787, America's business-minded people saw the potential for something big happening and didn't want to be left out.

Between 1776 and 1783, while the Revolutionary War was fought and the Articles of Confederation authored, America's elite was motivated by traditional business practices. Not until peace was attained and the depression deflated their standards of living did America's elite look for more profit-generating options. The pieces began making sense to them: machines doing the labor, steam generating the energy, coal and iron replacing wood, etc. The world was beginning to look like one huge factory that would generate riches and wealth that were heretofore unimaginable, and their newly liberated country, the United States of America, was going to be one of the major cogs.

VII. Adam Smith

Adam Smith was born in England to relatively well-off parents. He never experienced life from the point of view of a peon, living a life of relative leisure and good fortune (even though he was a rather sickly child). After reaching adulthood, he became a teacher and freelance lecturer and, over time, developed his theories of economic liberty.

Smith denounced interventionist governments as unnatural and advocated the establishment of a free enterprise market economy. This free enterprise market economy would govern itself because responsible and self-commanding people of high moral and aesthetic quality would resist the call of greed and realize that satisfying the consumer was the key to profits and economic stability. Because the market was free, Smith reasoned, it would naturally be just.

In 1776, a few months before the American colonies declared their independence, Adam Smith published <u>The Wealth of Nations</u>. In this book, he laid out his argument for a free enterprise market economy and criticized government restrictions and trade monopolies as barriers to economic activity. To Smith, America was the perfect spot to test out his theories.

There were at least three fallacies in Smith's arguments. Number one is the nature of business-centric humans. Business-centric individuals are not responsible and self-commanding people of high moral and aesthetic quality who resist the call of greed. To the contrary, business-centric individuals are greedy people; their driving ambition is to make money and more money and, in their minds, the ends they seek always justify the means they make use of. Secondly, Smith did not have an adequate understanding of the nature of a business-centric system. A business-centric system, like a political system, becomes an institution in and of itself. As such, part of its maturing process is the establishment of its own preservation as its primary objective. It is incapable of maintaining a balanced perspective of its relevance, and must, of necessity, be controlled by external forces. Thirdly, Smith apparently did not understand capitalism, the economic force that was maturing and making an impact on a newly developing world market. Upon cursory review, capitalism resembles free enterprise but is, in fact, its complete opposite. Capitalism does not operate within the confines of a free enterprise market economy. Quite to the contrary, capitalism is characterized by eliminating the competition, which, in turn, eliminates the free market. Additionally, capitalism cares little about satisfying the consumer in a way that is palatable to the consumer. Without the proper restraints, it would enslave the mass of consumers, subject them to a general state of poverty and, eventually, either crumble under the weight of its own vices or generate levels of inequity and iniquity that could undermine all forms of human organization.

Whereas most of Europe responded to The Wealth of Nations lukewarmly, America's elites, upon getting hold of it, took it to heart. The more they felt the effects of the depression that followed the end of the war, the longer they held onto the government securities that could not be cashed in, and the more the Articles frustrated their financial schemes and efforts to expand into other markets, the more fervently they identified "government restrictions" as the culprit. Soon, they were initiating steps aimed at creating a government that would be responsive to the free market economy that would serve their interests. The Articles of Confederation, the constitution they had agreed to that had been almost ideal only a few years earlier, was now an impediment of monstrous proportions. Grave changes were called for, and selected portions of Adam Smith's book provided America's elites with the ammunition they needed to promote their expanded economic objectives.

VIII. Wall Street

In 1664, British warships entered New York's harbor. New York, then a Dutch colony that was called New Amsterdam, had become so prosperous that Great Britain had decided to take it from the Netherlands. With that act of military thievery (disguised as a reward of war), elements of business savvy and degrees of commercial speculation and fanaticism were added to the American business landscape that would intoxicate the Northern colonies, separate the entire colonies from Great Britain, militarily conquer the South and set its sight on corralling the rest of the world.

The colony of New Amsterdam was one huge shop; it was intended to be a money making machine, the people who ventured there had one thing in mind-- making money, and no hypocritical lining existed that tried to hide the fact that making money was the only reason for the colony's existence. In New Amsterdam, any type of government that did anything to obstruct business was bad government, and there was little, if any, of that. Instead, there were insurance companies, virtually unregulated banking, stock exchanges, limited liability corporations, joint stock companies and credit agencies. There were masters of financial innovation, get rich quick proposals and schemes, geniuses of finance, brilliant thieves, big-eyed morons and enough opportunities to make almost anybody think that he could become a rich man. Any idea, any activity, whether borne of the business community or not, could be viewed in financial terms, reduced to financial equations and marketed as the next cash cow.

New Amsterdam's headquarters, the center of its financial frenzy, was Wall Street. At the core of Wall Street were brokers and professional investors. A broker was a middleman, a wheeler-dealer; someone who could find parties that were in search of similar types of transactions and bring them together. With brokers, anything, literally ANY THING, could be the basis of a buy, sell or trade transaction. Given the nature of racism and the large number of slaves in New York, it is not surprising, then, that the first "commodity" regularly traded on Wall Street was Black men, women and children.

The professional investors on Wall Street resigned themselves to the likelihood of being poor one day, rich the next and in debt prison the third. They relished the uncertainty; the prospect of big profits was risky business! With a mindset intoxicated by big egos, big numbers and big expectations, the risk increased the allure rather than diminished it. The risk also made professional investors more prone to let the ends justify the means. To them, the money making theatre of operations was a financial battlefield. As in war, casualties (victims of scams, loss of fortunes, the pilfering of non-professional investors, etc) were an integral part of the process.

It was on Wall Street, in this wheeling dealing environment made up of self-interested individuals, among this "the ends justify the means" mind set, that a securities market evolved that enabled America's business elite to raise the monies needed to finance any business idea that a smart, roguish or hapless mind could imagine. By the late 1700s, it became clear that Wall Street's securities market could provide the necessary start-up capital for much more than companies. If given the required liberty, Wall Street could capitalize a complete industrial revolution.

If given the required liberty, Wall Street could capitalize the Industrial Revolution and turn a lot of elitist inclined individuals into millionaires. The Articles of Confederation, the agreed upon law of the land, would not provide the required degree of liberty, nor could it be converted to accommodate a government that revolved around political capitalism. It was an obstacle that had to be pushed to the side. The Articles of Confederation had to be eliminated.

CHAPTER EIGHTEEN:
THE OVERTHROW OF
THE AMERICAN REVOLUTION

I. The Articles of Confederation (1781-1787)

Between the time the war began and ended, the new country was governed by constitutional congresses and, beginning in 1781, the Articles of Confederation. While we hear quite a bit about the activities of the constitutional congresses, we hear comparatively little about the Articles of Confederation and the presidents that served the country between 1781 and 1787. Why?

Like its usurper (the present United States constitution), the Articles of Confederation was not close to being a democratic document. As far from being democratic as it was, it still proved to be too close to democracy to suit the men who were emerging as America's leaders. Why was it too close to democracy? Because too many of America's elites had the power to keep it from being amended without justifiable cause. In the eyes of many of America's elites, the reasons given by those who suggested that the Articles of Confederation was a fundamentally flawed document simply did not hold water.

The country could have profited from the Industrial Revolution with the Articles as its constitution because the Articles of Confederation could be amended. Article 13 of the Articles makes this clear. I quote:

"Every State shall abide by the determination of the United States in Congress assembled, on all questions which by this confederation are submitted to them. And the Articles of this Confederation shall be inviolably observed by every State, and the Union shall be perpetual; nor shall any alteration at any time hereafter be made in any of them; unless such alteration be agreed to in a Congress of the United States, and be afterwards confirmed by the legislatures of every State."

Thus, when the Congress made a general determination, every state was bound to abide by it. If Congress had agreed to amend the Articles so that it would become a more business-centric constitution and the United States government would be a more business-centric government, the states would have been obligated to go along with that determination. However, every amendment to the Articles required confirmation "by the legislatures of every state." It was the members of these legislatures, elitists in their own right, who were relatively satisfied with the present law of the land. Might they have been receptive to amendments? Probably. Might they have been receptive to one that would diminish states' rights in order to make the constitution more business centric? Definitely not!

II. Amending a Constitution

We must keep in mind: Amending a constitution is not an easy or speedy process. Proponents of the Equal Rights Amendment toiled for 50 years before they could get Congress to approve it in 1972. Thirty years later, at the time of this writing, it has still not been ratified by the required number of states. As such, it remains a proposed amendment to the United States constitution, not an enacted one. The case of the ERA might be an extreme one, but the rule is that constitutional amendments follow a four stage process that usually consumes quite a bit of time.

The first stage is an educational period that informs the public and legislators of the need for the amendment. Secondly, there is a legislative period that revolves around activities leading up to the discussion and approval of the amendment by Congress. Thirdly, there is a ratification period wherein each state discusses the amendment and votes to approve it. And finally, there is a post ratification delay. After the required number of states have approved or ratified the amendment, a determination is made as to when the amendment will become effective. Not only can it take years to complete all of these stages, it can take years to complete each of them.

To see how this might work, let's look at amendments to the present U. S. constitution. Article 11 was proposed to Congress in March of 1794, but not ratified until January, 1798; a period of nearly four years. Article 14 was proposed in June of 1866 and ratified in July of 1868, a full two years later. Article 16 was approved in July, 1909, but not ratified until February, 1913, nearly 33 months later. The process does not always take two to four years, but making fundamental changes to the law of the land is usually designed to be a lengthy process. Care goes into the formation of a constitution; that is, creating a substantial document that delicately balances the dissimilar interests of all of its relevant parties. A change to that document is not a matter to be taken lightly; it must be arduously scrutinized and adjusted in a way that does not destroy the balance that made the agreement possible.

America's business elites who wanted a more business friendly law of the land not only wanted to undo the very nature of the Articles of Confederation, they wanted to undo it immediately. Allowing the legislative process to proceed according to the method spelled out by the law would have been too time consuming to suit them. That process could have taken decades. They wanted conditions favorable to their objectives, and they wanted them quickly. If they could not get what they needed by abiding by the law, they were willing to ignore the law or supplant the law.

It has been said that rules are good when you run out of brains. It can't be alleged that America's business elite had run out of brains. They could have reasoned that what applied to rules also applied to laws, and what applied to laws also applied to constitutions (the law of the land). The law of the land, as it existed at that time, did not serve their purpose. Having plenty of brains, they reasoned that they could ignore the law. Recognizing that actions are critical to implementing changes, they usurped power, supplanted the existing constitution and replaced it with a constitution that would better serve their interests.

III. Some Business Men Meet

During the first years of the country's existence, meetings that revolved around commercial problems afflicting the nation's business men were frequent. One such meeting initiated steps that led to the Philadelphia assemblage and the writing of a new constitution. The American Revolution that had been started and completed by older men for traditional business and political reasons was on the way to being overthrown by mostly younger men with current and different business and political priorities.

Under the Articles, neighboring states were constantly arguing over economic matters. In March, 1785, arguments over the fishing and oyster industries along the Potomac River and Chesapeake Bay led to a meeting of committees from Virginia and Maryland. A decision was made to call another meeting and invite all of the states to discuss commercial problems faced by the country. As a result, delegates from five states met in Annapolis in 1776. Two of the delegates, Alexander Hamilton and James Madison, convinced the others that a larger, more inclusive meeting was necessary because something needed to be done to make the Articles fit the needs of the Union. In 1787, Congress heeded the call of the Annapolis meeting and invited all of the states to send delegates to Philadelphia "for the sole purpose of revising the Articles of Confederation." Congress' word legitimized the meeting and prompted the states to select delegates.

Congress' instructions did not call for the writing of a new constitution. The men who met in Philadelphia did not intend to amend the old one.

IV. A Constitutional Coup d'Etat

Prior to meeting in Philadelphia, many of America's young elites had already concluded that amending the Articles was not in the best interest of business. An undesirable buggy, even when repaired and made to look more appealing, was still an undesirable buggy. It was not likely to function as efficiently as one made to order. In addition, America's young elites realized that the amendment ratification process would be divisive and time consuming, and would probably end in defeat. It could open old wounds and generate new ones that could put the nation at risk. That, they concluded, was definitely not the road to take.

America's young elites had also given previous consideration to actually dissolving the Union. That, needless to say, was out of the question. The Union had to remain intact because it was the combination of states that made the country so promising. Therefore, when the delegates met, enough of them understood that their mission was not to improve the Articles, but to replace it with a new constitution. The decision to keep the proceedings of the meeting secret should have signalled that intent. They didn't want anything made public until they had worked out a solution that was acceptable to and would be eloquently defended by enough of the delegates.

That solution was unveiled in September, 1787. It consisted of a preamble and seven articles, and should have been submitted to Congress for review. It wasn't. Instead, it declared that ratification of the new constitution by nine of the thirteen states would make it the new law of the land. It further declared that the ratification process would not be carried out by existing state legislatures (those who were most likely to vote against the document) but by new, popularly elected state conventions. Thus, in a stroke, the Philadelphia delegates, without the authority to do so, had written a new constitution, changed the established ratification procedure and submitted it to state "conventions" for approval! The existing federal government, the government that had called for the meeting to amend the Articles, was ignored, undermined and supplanted. A coup d'etat, an overthrow of the national government, was taking place. But instead of putting up a fight and standing up for the integrity of the existing constitution, the existing Congress meekly acceded, formally submitted the new proposal to the states, and faded into the sunset. Less than 10 months later, 721 men in nine states (out of a total population of millions of people) had voted in favor of the new document. That made it the new law of the land. On the first Wednesday in March, 1789, it went into effect. The coup d'etat had succeeded.

The structural differences between the new constitution and the Articles of Confederation were not fundamental in nature. If political adjustments had been all that was needed, the buggy could have been repaired to satisfactorily serve the purpose. But the new constitution gave priority to commerce, not politics. America's new elites wanted the federal government to have the power to determine how business would be conducted in the United States of America. Congress had to have the authority to protect private property, issue money, assess taxes and regulate interstate commerce. This had not been possible under the Articles of Confederation, and the entire process of generating a new constitution was to insure that that shortcoming be corrected.

The opponents of the new constitution did not have to be told that a coup d'etat had taken place. They might not have used that term, but they loudly complained that it had been secretly fashioned and the delegates had exceeded their powers. Additionally, opponents recognized that the new constitution was essentially a business oriented document. Not only had it been secretly drawn up, they pointed out, but it had been secretly drawn up by representatives of a "propertied aristocracy;" and, after publication, promoted by businessmen, financial interests, professionals, influential members of the media and other moneyed elements. Added to that, opponents continued, was the fact that the rights of property were emphasized, but the rights of the every day man were held in such low esteem that there was not a single provision ("bill of rights") that would protect people from the excesses of the federal government or businesses.

The omission of a bill of rights was a deliberate omission. At the time the new constitution was written, every state constitution contained a bill of rights in one or another manner. That is because the state constitutions were somewhat political in nature. The new, federal constitution was business centric; it strictly observed the young elite's interpretation of Adam Smith. They did not want to codify or lend the law's backing to any concept that might interfere with the free flow of business. Human beings who could point to the law of the land to substantiate their rights could legally fight against the excesses of business and be an impediment to commercial progress. No impediment to business was desirable.

The framers of the new constitution had no intention of including a bill of rights when they met, vehemently opposed the idea after its absence was pointed out by opponents, and still had not included a bill of rights when the new constitution went into effect. Their primary concern was not "We, the people," it was, "We, the business people."

V. And States Rights???

The creators of the Articles of Confederation were obsessed with keeping the states independent and in control of their own affairs. To protect the rights of the states in general, the Articles provided for a weak central government. And, to protect the rights of the Southern states in particular, the Articles made it impossible for any government to take any action against slavery or the slave trade.

The experiences of conducting the Revolutionary War and living under the Articles of Confederation gradually convinced elites throughout the states that a strong central government was better able to run a country than a collective of strong state governments. With this realization, the concept of states rights began to transform itself. The makers of the American Revolution had been concerned about the potential abuses of a strong central government, so they wrote a constitution that recognized the supremacy of the states. Now, in the presence of radically changing economic realities, it was time to admit that a strong federal government was more beneficial than strong state governments. What the makers of the revolution had fought for could no longer be considered a driving priority. Other considerations, namely new business realities, had rendered states rights negligible.

The concept of states rights, then, began to ride off into the American sunset. It quickly rode through the Northern and Middle states, but when it entered the South it came to a screeching halt. The South, like the Northern and Middle states, was now in favor of a strong central government, but the economic realities of the South differed from those of the others. The South had to be assured that the federal government would not tamper with the system of labor that drove Southern capitalism. Henceforth, even though states rights was no longer the de facto issue (protecting the institution of slavery was), that term would be used as if it were the issue. From that point on, the states rights argument would take on a purely economic flavor and take expression in a predominantly Southern context.

In Chapter 14, I wrote about sectional incompatibilities that existed prior to the Revolutionary War. The incompatibility "that would have done more than anything else to keep the colonies from uniting revolved around the issue of labor. Southern businessmen would never have willingly formed a union with Northern businessmen because they could not trust Northerners to respect their system of labor." This same distrust persisted when the delegates met in Philadelphia in 1787. If it were not addressed in a manner that was favorable to the South, it would have been impossible to replace the Articles of Confederation with a new, more business centric law of the land.

The new constitution, by its very nature, was a guarantor of a changing and ever expanding Northern capitalism. That was understood by anyone who considered himself in the know. To satisfy Southerners, the new constitution had to also be a guarantor of Southern capitalism.
In order to make sure that the foundation of their business activities would not be tampered with, the "state
rights" of the South had to be written into the new constitution. The new constitution, like the old one, had to
be a pro-slavery constitution, a pro-slavery law of the
land.

VI. A Pro-Slavery Law of the Land

The term slavery does not appear a single time in the
constitution that was adopted to replace the Articles of
Confederation. Yet, the entire document, all seven Articles, reeks of that staple of the Southern economy.
Section 2 of Article 1 stipulates that "other persons,"
the code word for slaves, should be counted as 3/5 of a
man for purposes of representation. Section 9 of Article
1 also addresses "other persons," and in so doing pro-
tects the African slave trade and restricts the states from
directly taxing Southern planters for more than 3/5 of
their slave population. That Article also denies the states
the power to assess trade duties on products produced
by slave labor. Section 2 of Article 4 requires the entire
country to return fugitive slaves to their owners, and
Article 5 prohibits any amendment to the African slave
trade clause before the year 1808. [To demonstrate how
misleading a law can be, nothing occurred after 1808
that appreciably interfered with the African slave trade.
The tone of the law suggested that it would be eliminated.]

And there is more. Other protections for the economic lifeline of the South that look political in essence
are woven throughout the new "law" of the land. There
is a guarantee of federal support in case of "insurrec-

tions" (the code word for slave rebellions) that obligates the entire country to go to war if the slaves should attempt to overthrow that institution. There is the creation of an electoral college whose major intent was to give the Southern states an upper hand in the balloting for president. There is also a 3/4 ratification clause to make sure that the Southern states could defeat any proposed amendment to the constitution that they didn't like (It was assumed that any such amendment would be economic in nature). And on top of that, Congress, which was empowered to control all forms of interstate commerce, was denied the power to control commercial activities that were related to slavery. Slavery and the slave trade, the most national and international of economic realities, were defined as "domestic institutions" for that reason and that reason alone.

To those who argue that these were political concessions, it must be understood that none of them would have existed if it were not for the necessity of protecting the lifeline of the Southern economy. If it were not for economic considerations that were unique to the South, there never would have been an electoral college, a fugitive slave clause, a 3/5 provision, a ratification clause that requires approval by 3/4 of the states, or any exceptions made to Congress' control of interstate commerce. The new constitution was, first and foremost, an economic document, and the concessions made to accommodate the Southern economy clearly, unmistakably, bear this out.

Curiously, the constitution's treatment of slavery makes the case for another cornerstone of business oriented realities; that being the total disrespect for and lack of regard for labor. The provisions of the new constitution that protected Southern slavery were not only an attack on slave labor, it was an attack on labor in general. One of the keys to maximizing profit is paying as little as possible for labor. The constitution's protection of slave labor, then, is another pat on business' back. Would an essentially political document address the issue of labor like that? I doubt it. But an essentially economic document would, so the new United States constitution did.

Section Three: Summary

The colonies that were to become the United States of America were essentially business entities, and they prospered the same way businesses generally prosper. Underpaid labor, most notably in the form of slaves, was the biggest operating expense that was never paid. There was also the discovery of money crops, money products and money services that people were willing to pay for on a repeated basis. Efficiency of operations, as much then as today, was much talked about but rarely in evidence.

Nonetheless, the colonies began to prosper. With prosperity came discord because of disagreements about how the prosperity should be shared. Quite importantly, colonial discontentment was not restricted to the colonies vis a vis Great Britain. Sectional incompatibilities within the colonies were so fundamental in nature that the presence of Great British, frequently, was the only thing that kept the colonies from warring against each other. These incompatibilities were, for the most part, put to the side while the colonies fought the Revolutionary War and gained their political independence.

After gaining independence, the colonists agreed to a national constitution. It was called the Articles of Confederation. The Articles represented the business and political priorities of the makers of the American Revolution. Within only a few years, younger men with different priorities carried out a constitutional coup d'etat. Without the authority to do so, they drafted a new constitution and implemented a process that resulted in their constitution supplanting the Articles of Confederation (the legitimate constitution). With this constitutional coup d'etat, the American revolution came to an end and a new country "of business, by business and for business" rose its runted and single-minded head.

Section Three: Review Questions

(1) Is it probable that Black People and Red People coexisted harmoniously in the Americas before the arrival of white people? Explain.

(2) Is it accurate to say that Cristobal Colon (Christopher Columbus) discovered America? If not, why does that continue be taught in America's schools?

(3) Did the Catholic Church and white governments work hand in hand in the extermination of Native Americans and the enslavement of Black People? Support your contention.

(4) What were the key factors that made the colonies prosperous?

(5) Did the white people who colonized and settled the new world know it was wrong to enslave Black People?

(6) How did white individuals and the white world benefit from the enslavement of Black People?

(7) Underpaid labor was a cornerstone of the wage policies advocated by Northern businessmen and opponents of slavery. Explain how that is the case.

(8) What was the major difference between the English colonies and the Dutch colony of New Amsterdam?

(9) There was discontentment between the colonies and Great Britain. What was at the heart of that discontentment?

(10) There were incompatibilities within the colonies, particularly between those in the South and North, that kept them at odds with one another. What was at the heart of these incompatibilities?

(11) What was at the source of British aggression in the 1770s, and what impact did this have on the colonies?

(12) What is the relevance of Pontiac's War to the American REvolution?

(13) Slogans like "taxation without representation" and complaints about a standing army were too weak to

motivate the settlers to seek independence from Great Britain. What, in fact, was strong enough to drive the American settlers to that end?

(14) From the standpoint of American businessmen, what was the advantage of separating from Great Britain?

(15) Was business the real reason the American Revolution was fought?

(16) Why did everyday settlers carry the burden of the war even though they did not stand to benefit in any fundamental way from the war?

(17) In your opinion, would the elite classes have fought the war so that everyday people might have benefitted?

(18) Was the American Revolution a revolution or a coup d'etat? Support your position.

(19) Did the American settlers have a reasonable chance of winning the American Revolutionary War?

(20) Were the American colonies prepared to fight a war against Great Britain?

(21) What is meant by the following passage: "Historical developments are much more than paper predictions, much more than research, analysis and logical conclusions. History is the harnessing and release of varying degrees of energy, and logic is not the only powerful factor that needs to be taken into account."

(22) What did the American colonists discover as the war with Great Britain progressed?

(23) What do you think about the following passage: "The Americans did not defeat the British, but they placed their destiny into their own hands, took on the responsibilities winners take on and emerged victorious."

(24) What is a provisional government?

(25) What is the Articles of Confederation?

(26) Who is John Hanson? In your opinion, was John Hanson the first president of the United States of America? Explain.

(27) Was the Articles of Confederation a hastily drawn up constitution?

(28) Was the Articles of Confederation a business centric constitution?

(29) Was the Articles of Confederation a pro-slavery constitution?

(30) Did the Articles of Confederation champion a strong central government?

(31) Was the Articles of Confederation problematic for everyday people?

(32) Was the Articles of Confederation problematic for business conscious people?

(33) Were the shortcomings of the Articles of Confederation economically or politically based?

(34) In your opinion, would everyday citizens have called for the replacement of the Articles of Confederation? Explain.

(35) Could the Articles of Confederation have been amended to make it a more efficient and business centric constitution?

(36) Would the United States of America have stood still if the Articles of Confederation had remained the law of the land?

(37) The phrase "The Straws that Stirred the Milkshake" was used. What does the term "milkshake" refer to, and what were the straws that stirred it?

(38) What role did the Industrial Revolution play in the replacement of the Articles of Confederation with a new constitution?

(39) What role did Adam Smith play in the replacement of the Articles of Confederation with a new constitution? What were some of the fallacies in Adam Smith's writings?

(40) What is Wall Street? What role did Wall Street play in the replacement of the Articles of Confederation with a new constitution?

(41) Did the supplanting of the Articles of Confederation by a new constitution equate to a constitutional coup d'etat?

(42) Did the supplanting of the Articles of Confederation by a new constitution indicate the end of the

American Revolution?

(43) Did the writers of the new constitution abide by the law?

(44) What proof can you give to support the assertion that the new constitution was a business-centric document, not a political one?

(45) What was the response of everyday people to the supplanting of the Articles of Confederation by a new constitution?

(46) In the process of replacing the Articles of Confederation with a new constitution, what happened to the concept of states rights?

(47) Was the new constitution more or less business-centric than the Articles of Confederation?

(48) Was the new constitution fundamentally different from the Articles of Confederation as far as slavery was concerned?

(49) What ridiculous and/or unnecessary clauses clutter the new constitution that would not be there if the constitution had not been trying to protect the economic lifeline of the South?

Section 4:
THE LAW OF THE LAND

CHAPTER NINETEEN: A NATION STEEPED IN HYPOCRISY

I. Introduction

Since it is function that defines essence, it is correct to conclude that the United States constitution was driven by commercial concerns, not political or human ones. From the very beginning, because of the ground in inclinations of the people who stole the land from the Native Americans and the nature of their institutions, the colonies were destined to battle with contradictions between what they professed and what they actually practiced. The United States, then, was steeped in fundamental contradictions at its birth; contradictions which, in most cases, preceded the white people who were to come to these shores. However, when the United States overthrew the legally established law of the land and supplanted it with one that professed free enterprise and liberty for all, it augured a nation that would be increasingly enamored of deceit and guided by hypocrisy. From that point on, rather than confront those debilitating tendencies and try to expunge or ameliorate them, the new nation negligently rested its principles on them. As the nation grew territory by territory and state by state, deceit and hypocrisy exponentially entrenched themselves and evolved into major underpinnings of "Americanism."

II. Out With the Vanquished

The first constitution of the United States of America was the Articles of Confederation. In a country where the importance of roots is given so much lip service, it seems strange that the Articles and the offices that were sanctioned and served under it do not occupy a sacred place, a relatively hallowed place, in America's textbooks and lore. Quite to the contrary, it has been conspicuously under-mentioned, almost unofficially deleted, from white America's heritage. Why is the government that ran the country through the early years of the country's infancy treated so disdainfully?

Students who develop an understanding of both United States history and the men who seized control of the new country are not puzzled by this at all. In the same manner that the white men who seized control of the American Revolution did not hold King George or his government in high esteem, the men who overthrew the American Revolution did not hold the government under the Articles of Confederation in high esteem. Part of their victory involved obliterating the memory of and burying that which they had vanquished. The first generation of Americans vanquished King George, and the second generation of Americans vanquished the government the first generation of Americans had established. In both cases a revolution, or more accurately, a coup d'etat, had taken place. The only difference is that the first, which involved gunfire and the participation of everyday people, LOOKED LIKE an overthrow of the government. The second, which involved certain white men and no gunfire, did not.

But appearances are frequently misleading. When one digs down to the origin of the new constitution, one finds the ingredients that go into the making of a coup d'etat and the reactionary cleansing process that follows (if it succeeds). The virtual deletion of the Articles of Confederation, its presidents, its accomplishments and its basic consistency with the constitution that replaced it are victims of this cleansing process. Once cleansed, the Articles would be less talked about. Once less talked about, it would be less likely suggested that the new constitution became the law of the land as a result of illegalities. In turn, that would preclude discussions based on the premise that the most cherished heroes of this country were gangs of co-conspirators who overthrew a legitimate republican government and replaced it with one that was less republican and of less benefit to the people of this country.

The fact that the new constitution was simply a later model, an "improved" version, of the Articles of Confederation was lost in the zeal of the men who supplanted it. It was their preference that the first baby drown in and be thrown out with the bath water. They were intent on not only making a daring statement, but leaving a noble impression. Anything that might generate doubt about either had to be totally-- completely-- removed from the picture.

III. Political Continuity

The baby went out with the bath water but, politically speaking, the transition from the Articles of Confederation to the new constitution was not a transition at all. Instead, it was a continuation. There was never a permeating mood of political doubt that might be converted into an appreciable level of political instability. And, as far as fundamental and guiding principles are concerned, the new constitution, politically speaking, did not differ from the Articles at all. If addressed in fairy tale terms, it could be said that the new constitution was the same species of wolf as the old, but it was dressed to look like Alice's grandmother.

One would have difficulty uncovering political priorities and policies established by government under the Articles that were undone by the government that was installed under the new constitution. Even as the new constitution was being ratified, the Congress that had been installed by the Articles was approving the Northwest Ordinance. From a political standpoint, the Northwest Ordinance determined how the territories in the Northwest would be governed and converted into new states. However, the Northwest Ordinance also prohibited slavery in those territories. Under the new constitution, that provision of the Northwest Ordinance would have been nullified because Congress did not have the power to regulate business that was slavery related. No such nullification was called for, however, because the intent of the drafters of the Northwest Ordinance was the same as that of the drafters of the new constitution. The prohibition against slavery in the Northwest Territory was not a political statement or a strike against slavery! Quite to the contrary, it was a pro-slavery initiative that was aimed at protecting the economic interests of established Southern businessmen. It did just that.

Politically speaking, the Northwest Ordinance is proof that the Articles of Confederation and the government it established had the ability to satisfactorily address the political needs of the nation. In fact, it did address those needs until it was faded away by frenzied economic priorities. It can not be overstated: the new constitution was an economics driven document, not a political one. The economic differences between the Articles and the new constitution were vital, and the changes imposed by the new constitution in that respect had an immediate impact. The political changes, on the other hand, were essentially cosmetic. Like everything that is essentially cosmetic, they seized the attention but otherwise were largely meaningless.

IV. A New Government

The coup d'etat carried out by the makers of the U. S. constitution proves that, at its barest, revolution is not a matter of gunfire but of who controls each individual's personal power. The younger men who wrote the new constitution knew that when one gives his or her power to a government that fails to function in the desired manner, one can always repossess his or her power; that is, take it from the undesirable government and give it to one that is more accommodating. Consistent with that understanding, they repossessed their power and created a union that was "more perfect" for them.

The debate over the new constitution that took place prior to its ratification produced two major political advocacies. One was called the Federalists, and the other Anti-federalists. According to traditional books on American history, the Federalists were those who believed in a strong central government. It might be more appropriate to say that the Federalists believed in a government that gave free reign to business and business related activities. Quite importantly, the Anti-Federalists believed in a strong central government also, but were concerned that it might overstep its boundaries.

After working together to make the new constitution the law of the land, the supporters of the new constitution split into two groups because they disagreed on the extent to which the law of the land could be used to impose the economic preferences of Northern capitalism onto the rest of the nation, particularly the South. Based on this disagreement, two political parties emerged. The ones who pushed for Northern style economic dominance called themselves Federalists, and were led by Alexander Hamilton. The other party was led by Thomas Jefferson, with its members alternately known as Jeffersonians and Democratic-Republicans, and was preoccupied with protecting the basis of Southern capitalism. In this way, the two party system reared its head in the United States. Those same two parties, going through a variety of name changes and variations, have totally dominated and continue to dominate American politics to this day.

Alexander Hamilton and Thomas Jefferson, along with George Washington, have been celebrated as the greatest of white America's founding fathers. A fourth, James Madison, was just as important to the development of the new nation. Hamilton and Madison were, by far, the most forward looking of the group; Hamilton focussing on economics and Madison on politics. George Washington, the most politically naive, was also the most essential. That leaves Thomas Jefferson, the most celebrated of them all. Students of white history typically call Jefferson a visionary. That might have been. What is certain is that Thomas Jefferson was a polished hypocrite.

In a nation steeped in hypocrisy and dominated by insidiousness, Thomas Jefferson might well be the most hypocritical white man of national prominence this country has ever known. His enormous popularity says volumes about the subconscious inclinations of the people in the country he helped rear.

V. The Pillars of Hypocrisy

Alexander Hamilton had a vision of the United States as a driving economic force in a rapidly developing industrial world. In order to reach its business potential, Hamilton recognized the need for a federal government that controlled all of the keys to the economic development of the nation. With that in mind, Hamilton helped initiate the push for a new constitution. After seeing the new constitution ratified, Hamilton acted as George Washington's Secretary of the Treasury. In that capacity, he successfully funded the national debt AT FACE VALUE (which put money into the pockets of speculators who had bought bonds at a discounted price from those who had financially bankrolled the Revolutionary War), created the first national bank (which increased the chances that investors in America's new government would recover their investment if things didn't go well) and pushed for close ties with Great Britain (the center of capitalist development in Europe). Hamilton wanted a government that was operated by the few and business-centric. In the long run, his objective was realized moreso than those of his opponents.

Hamilton, an elitist to the core, could not or would not see that a business centric government based in a free enterprise system is not the same as one based in capitalism. Thus, instead of promoting a healthy business environment driven by hard work, healthy competition and "gaining an honest dollar," Hamilton in fact promoted a business environment that was driven by the type of financial frenzy, "make a dollar at all costs" bigotry and cutthroat monopolizing that is typical of Wall

Street. Hamilton, then, was the major initiator of America's financial machine. That machine broke all reins and went on to dishearten even Hamilton and thoroughly corrupt the young country he loved.

What Hamilton was to the economic development of the country, James Madison was to its political development. Madison was the single most important person to actually play a role in the writing of the new constitution. He saw clearly where he wanted the country to go and what he wanted the country to represent, and he successfully passed his vision on to the other delegates in Philadelphia. After the constitution was ratified, Madison drafted laws and interpreted provisions that transformed the constitution from words on paper into a tangible, operating economic and political machine. Without Madison, the process in Philadelphia might have proved to be too inertia prone and might have been doomed to failure.

Madison supposedly wanted a government that rested on the people rather than the states. He saw the federal government as the only vehicle that could be used to represent the will of all of the country's people, and crafted a constitution to that end. But, Madison's argument in favor of the people was deceitful and misleading; it was invoked primarily to sidestep the ratification process called for by the Articles of Confederation. If "the people" had been his concern, he would have argued for a constitution that empowered the people and he would not have allowed a constitution to be introduced that did not include a Bill of Rights. What Madison really wanted was a more efficient form of government that would function in the interests of a select few. The new constitution served the purpose in that regard.

George Washington was a member of the old guard, belonging to the generation that preceded those of Jefferson, Hamilton and Madison. Washington was not only the least politically astute of the four, but of most of the men who participated in the American Revolution. However, compared to his contemporaries, George Washington was an extremely honest and trustworthy person.

These two traits gave other men the impression that they could get a square deal from him, and resulted in them being more tolerant and open to compromise with him than their other contemporaries. Because he was considerably taller than most men of his day, Washington satisfied the physical image that people have of a leader. For that reason as much as any (he did not have a good military career), Washington was chosen as Commander in Chief of the Revolutionary Army. He was incapable of winning that war, but he was capable of holding the army together until Great Britain was collapsed by its lack of commitment to the war effort.

Washington was elected the president of the constitutional convention, but he hardly did anything. It was his presence that counted; it made each of the delegates, who were mostly self-serving, feel that a solution could be worked out that was equitable to each of them. As long as Washington was in charge, each delegate felt confident that everyone's concerns would be given the consideration they deserved. For this same reason, the electoral college chose George Washington as the first president of the country under the new constitution. There was simply no one else that many of the other elite individuals trusted.

As President, George Washington didn't have a political platform. Since he never "ran" for the office, he did not have to present a program to the voters. Once elected, Washington picked among the best ideas and suggestions of his zealous cabinet members. He supported the free enterprise elements of Alexander Hamilton's program, but he did not support its capitalist elements (those that favored manufacturing and Wall Street type activities). Although classified as a Federalist, Washington did not understand the need for political parties. This was indicative of his sincere dedication to the new country. Indicative of his slow rate of comprehension was the fact that he did not see that certain individuals were using and would forever use the country to advance their more trivial and self-serving objectives until his final years in office.

Based on what he wrote, Thomas Jefferson believed in the natural rights of people and of their capacity to govern. The most natural right was the right to self-government. According to his writings, Jefferson had faith in majority rule, believed that less government was better government, and also believed that the rights and civil liberties of the minority should be protected. But one cannot adequately judge Jefferson by what he wrote; what he spent his time working to bring about is a better indicator. When Jefferson really believed in something, one can see a courageous continuity between what he wrote and what he did. When he thought something was correct but was unwilling to take it seriously, he might write about it with speculative conviction but would never attempt to make it a reality. This enabled him to mislead or deceive his readers who, as readers are prone to do, took his writings at face value.

Not surprisingly, this type of flippant advocacies and speculative deception benefitted him immensely. For example, one of the reasons Jefferson was elected president was because of the support he received from slaveholders AND opponents of slavery. The slaveholders voted for him because he was a slave master. The opponents of slavery voted for him because his writings were frequently anti-slavery. In fact, Jefferson never did anything in support of his anti-slavery writings. By contrast, he defended the rights of slave owners and the institution of slavery vigorously and without hesitation. His actions, not his writings, were his defining statements. Yet he is remembered for his writings as much as anything.

Thomas Jefferson, probably more than any other single person, is representative of the hypocrisy and popularity of the United States of America. In order to get an accurate read on either, one must ignore the cosmetic indicators and concentrate on the deeds, what they invest their time and energy in. It is there that one can discover the truth about both, and determine the value of those truths.

In these four men is found the essential quality and character of the United States of America. Make no mistake: they were not the makers of the United States of America. Quite to the contrary, they were molded by the same forces that molded the United States of America. As a result, not one of them could resist the obvious sin of dehumanizing humanity and enslaving other human beings, nor could they resist other fundamental wrongs that fattened their wallets and furthered their ambitions. The one whose values were the least offensive, George Washington, was the least astute. Alexander Hamilton loved the country but could not have valued the people who fought to make the country free. To Hamilton, business affairs were more important than human affairs. James Madison talked about the welfare of the people but could not believe in their welfare enough to actually incorporate it into the law of the land. Consequently, Madison acted exclusively in the interests of the elite. And Thomas Jefferson, by far the most relished of the four, was unquestionably the most deceptive. If either of them had actually been committed to doing what was good for the people of this country, the coup d'etat of 1776, otherwise known as the American Revolution, might have matured into a genuinely revolutionary experiment in government by the people. But America's main men were too weak individually, too motivated by personal considerations and too based in a narrow view of humanity to take advantage of that opportunity. In short, they were not quite civilized enough to make the world a better place or accomplish anything of truly grand proportions. Unfortunately, the country they became symbolic of retained all of their inadequacies.

CHAPTER 20:
THE BUSINESS OF THE NATION

I. The Invisible Pilot

It is easy but inaccurate to attribute the country's direction after 1789 to persons such as George Washington, Thomas Jefferson and the like. The fact of the matter is this: the men responsible for the new constitution were motivated by an ideological infrastructure that assumed control of the constitution and the government they created. Consequently, the offices that were created to govern the country, including the presidency, are dominated by this ideological infrastructure; its objectives, its predispositions and its inclinations. This ideological infrastructure, via "the system," also monitors and regulates the individuals who serve as office holders. Therefore, individual office holders do not influence the offices inasmuch as the offices, via the system, influence them. What office holders should and should not do are systemically suggested. Even though different individuals will occupy an office, including the presidency, the tendencies that created the office prompt the office holder to work toward predisposed objectives and against all others. As a result, while a few office holders might test the system's ideological periphery, most stay close to its ideological center. Most importantly, almost none attempt to operate outside of the predisposed parameters. Each office holder must operate within those parameters because to do otherwise makes him/her vulnerable to being stripped of the authority generally accorded to the office s/he occupies.

In other words, each system has something akin to a genetic code. That code dictates what a system can and can not be. In spite of all of the high sounding proclamations about "the people," "the land of opportunity," "the land of liberty" and what the United States could be, the United States was only capable of being one thing; a greedy, arrogant, militaristic country that rotated around business considerations. From time to time, individuals would come along who tried to make the United States something other than that, something better than that, something more humane than that, but they couldn't. Thus, Cristobal Colon's fortuitous "discovery," characteristic greed and arrogance, lack of concern for the rights of others and ruthless cruelty unwittingly augured a fingerprint of and modus operandi for a country that was not to exist until nearly 300 years later-- the United States of America.

II. Office Holders and Policies

After the constitutional coup d'etat that supplanted the Articles of Confederation, a handful of men elected George Washington as president of the country. Under Washington, political activities took place that gave form and function to the new government both domestically and internationally. Domestically, the executive branch took form, the judicial branch was created, interpretations of the new constitution were made and judicial and administrative rulings were issued that made the constitution applicable to the everyday lives of everyday people. Means of generating federal revenue had to be established, a standard currency had to be agreed upon, rules of trade standardized and regulated, and rules of conduct between the states formalized. Internationally, a foreign policy was devised that revolved, for the overwhelming part, around the relationship of the United States to other white countries, principally Great Britain, France and Spain. In fact, if one were to eliminate the countries of Europe, the United States would not have needed a foreign policy at all between 1789 and 1940. The United States was not ignorant of or totally isolated from the non-European world, it simply did not accord the non-European world enough significance to establish policies in regard to it. The United States did participate in a large number of international activities during this time period that did not revolve around European countries. For instance, the United States government acted to protect merchant ships owned and operated by United States businessmen against Arabic seafarers. Additionally, the United States started a war with Mexico in order to assume ownership of Mexican territories. But random strokes and haphazard exchanges are not the stuff policies are made of. Policies, for the United States, were restricted to the maintenance of business and political dealings between and among white nations.

There are three notable exceptions to what was just stated. The United States did have a consistent stance toward the Black nation of Haiti. Immediately after the United States fought for and gained its independence from Great Britain, the Blacks in San Domingo fought for and gained their independence from France. The Blacks rejected the name San Domingo and renamed their country Haiti. It would have made sense for the new country of the United States to establish normal diplomatic relations with the new country of Haiti, particularly because they were so close to each other and could have been of so much mutual benefit. But Haiti was not a European or white country, it was a Black country. Consequently, the United States colluded with Spain, France and Great Britain to economically and politically isolate Haiti from the rest of the world. These white countries, in effect, established the policy of strangling the young Black nation and made it impossible for it to become anything but the politically and economically destitute cesspool that it is today. That is the general policy of white power toward Black power realities, and in the case of Haiti, the United States adhered to that policy without the least bit of serious vacillation.

It was more of the same as far as Africa and Native Americans were concerned. Africa was a source of free labor and, therefore, a key to America's prosperity. The United States' policy was to maintain that reality for as long as necessary. Native Americans constituted a nation of people who were the legitimate owners of the land the United States had assumed control of. The United

States' policy was to eliminate the Native American population to the extent that they could not lay politically viable claims to the land that had been robbed from them.

In addition to giving domestic and international form and function to the new government, Washington and his presidential successors had to attend to the long standing priorities and incompatibilities that had evolved since the settling of the early colonies. Before Washington's presidency, the 13 colonies and new nation were handicapped by sectional and labor system differences, national security issues and commercial anxieties that hinged on expansion into new territories. Coming to an accord over the labor system differences was a near impossibility, generating a civil war spark in the 1820s that burned incessantly until it exploded in the 1860s. The issues of national security revolved around British, Spanish and French land claims and trading posts in the Americas, and their treaties with Native Americans. All of these issues were addressed as part of the United States' foreign policy agenda. Even though Americans typically referred to protection against Native American raids as part of their security concerns, the fact of the matter is otherwise. Dealing with the Native Americans was not a question of security, but of economics. It wasn't the Native Americans' raids that concerned white America, it was the Native Americans' presence.

III. Political Parties

If political parties revolved around disagreements over fundamental issues, there would never have been a political party in the United States of America. White Americans agreed that the economic philosophy of the country should revolve around capitalism; no viable political party could emerge that advocated a fundamental economic alternative. White Americans agreed that the Native American populations should be eliminated; no viable political party could emerge that advocated a fundamental alternative to that solution. White America believed in what would later become known as manifest destiny; no viable political party could emerge that advocated a fundamental alternative to the continued expansion of the country into western territories. White America believed in what it called Christianity; no viable political party could emerge that worshipped the god(s) of a non-Christian religious ideology. And, white Americans believed in the white mythology. They believed that white people were superior to all other races of people, that white people had an inherently ordained right to rule and wield power, and that it was natural for white people to benefit and profit from the blood, sweat and tears of non-white peoples. As a consequence, in the United States of America, no viable political party could emerge that advocated the equality of all human beings, the right of non-white peoples to govern themselves or the fallacy of the white mythology.

After the new constitution was ratified, opposing forces emerged that disagreed over how much power the states should have within the agreed upon federal system and what the place of unpaid labor would be within the agreed upon economic system. The line was drawn over those issues, and two political parties emerged. From that point on, from 1789 until the present, the American political scene has been dominated by the same two political parties (even though the names change from time to time). However, the issue that was now being referred to as "state power" fizzled into a non-issue over time, and the issue of unpaid labor was resolved in the 1860s. Since that time, the two parties have had nothing of any substance to distinguish the one from the other, and have served little, if any, purpose of substance.

IV. The Political Parties Hoax: From Issues to Non-Issues

The followers of Alexander Hamilton and Thomas Jefferson started what has become a political party hoax. The followers of Hamilton believed that the constitution should be interpreted in a way that enabled the federal government to increase its powers without limits, while the followers of Jefferson believed the constitution should be interpreted in a way that increased the power of the states as much as possible, so long as it did not interfere with the ability of the federal government to carry out its mandate. The followers of Alexander Hamilton also believed that unpaid labor was a hindrance to American capitalism, while followers of Jefferson believed that un-paid labor was just as essential to American capitalism as paid labor. In the beginning, Hamilton's followers prevailed. The federal government succeeded in expanding its pow-ers, over-rewarding speculators who owned Revolution-ary War bonds and establishing a national bank that would facilitate Northern capitalism's efforts to finance and profit from the Industrial Revolution. England, the pre-miere capitalist country in the world, was courted by Fed-eralists as the European ally of choice. However, by the end of Washington's first term, the tide had begun to shift in favor of the Jeffersonians. John Adams, another Federalist, succeeded Washington as president, but had neither the support of Hamilton nor Jefferson. Adams' biggest accomplishment was to negotiate the removal of British troops from western territories. Four years af-ter Adams' election, Thomas Jefferson was chosen presi-dent. His election signaled an end to Hamilton's national bank, less expansion of federal power and the establish-ment of friendly relations with France, Britain's most pow-erful adversary.

This back and forth jockeying over non-fundamental issues typified politics in the United States for several decades, and continues today. It brought on and augured an American political system composed of political par-ties that are essentially indistinguishable and lobbying activities that are not political but economic and profit oriented. Such political processes do not revolve around the relationship of social institutions to human beings, but of governmental, commercial and religious market-ers to consumers. While the attention of the nation is focussed on the hectic public gyrations associated with city halls, capitol hills and executive mansions, the political processes that count proceed about the fundamental business of the nation stealthily, clandestinely, unremittingly. Just like the modus operandi of the framers of the new constitution, the modus operandi of the country's political process involves discussing the issues that count in relative secrecy, reaching critical decisions without public input or knowledge and authorizing courses of action in spite of the public's ignorance and in defiance of public disapproval. By conducting the political process in this way, the invisible pilot ensures that the average American citizen is unable to realize that "policies" that are supposed to be based on "national security" and "democracy" concerns are nothing more than the government use of the people's taxes and resources in the support of private business initiatives.

CHAPTER 21:
THE NATION AGES AND EXPANDS

I. America's Paradigm

What is most striking about George Washington's presidency is its consistency with America's past and future. America's paradigm, its central motivating forces, preceded Washington's presidency, absorbed it and outlived it. It did the same thing for all of America's presidencies. For that reason, it is wiser to concentrate primarily on the developments that took place in America and less on the roles certain men played in bringing about those developments.

II. Fair Weather Morals

Morals have not fitted into the fabric of the United States of America. That is not a vindictive or judgmental statement, it is simply a recognition of a fact. Americans give a great deal of lip service to the importance of treating human beings "humanely," " playing fair," and observing codes of proper conduct, but when push comes to shove, their morals lose steam and become the little choo choo that doesn't matter at all. This fact is crystal clear when one takes note of the fact that white Americans who wanted ownership of land that did not belong to them decided to terrorize and exterminate the Black and Red people who rightfully occupied it. It became crystal clear again when, instead of doing their own work or fairly paying someone else to do it, they ravaged the families and communities of Africa, kidnapped the strongest men, women and children and brought them to this country as slaves. And again, one can point to the totally immoral rape and possession of countries like Hawaii, Puerto Rico, Granada and the Philippines. In fact, at this precise moment, I cannot think of one instance where morality or humane considerations was the factor that determined white America's response to a crucial situation or set of circumstances. Morality, like religion, is simply not one of white America's central motivating forces. Individuals who want to understand the history of white America must accustom themselves to this reality.

[Note: I discuss central motivating forces in Chapter 1 of Ten Lessons: An Introduction to Black History. Reviewing that chapter will help the student of history better understand the development of white people, including white Americans.]

In Ten Lessons: An Introduction to Black History, I wrote that economics determines the politics, worship and social structure of the white world. Every value possessed by white America that does not have an economic essence is subject to be relegated to insignificance at any given time. Economics drives white America, economics is the only thing that really matters to white America, and economic considerations will, as a matter of course, inspire white America and white Americans to commit the most atrocious hostility against any other country or human being. Given that America started off as little businesses that were expressly geared toward making money, it is not surprising that such is the case. What is surprising is that, in spite of that, otherwise intelligent individuals think they can bring about change in white America by appealing to white America's conscience or making white America feel shameful about its conduct. There is nothing in the history of white America to suggest that an iota of validity resides in that assumption.

III. Westward Expansion

At the time the U. S. Constitution was being written, the United States Congress had authorized a commission to determine the process by which the Northwest territories should be organized, formed into states and entered into the Union. At that time, the Northwest, imprecisely speaking, was that land mass west of New York, Pennsylvania and Virginia, north of Tennessee and east of the Mississippi River. For more than a hundred years, the Native Americans who occupied this land had been under attack from white settlers. Land speculators wanted to make money exploiting the area in a number of ways, settlers wanted to make money by moving into that area and establishing homesteads and businesses, Southern planters wanted to make money by expanding their agricultural slavocracy into that area, Wall Street and Northern capitalists wanted to make money by expanding commercial production and developing additional consumer markets, and Congress wanted the various types of tax revenue that freeing the land of "Indians" and opening it to white Americans would generate. In July, 1787, on one of the days that might have been celebrated as Independence Day by white Americans, white lawmakers passed the Northwest Ordinance, which was a blueprint for American colonialism. With its passage, a modus operandi was established that defined how new territories acquired by the United States would be organized, made to recognize "law and order" and admitted to the Union as new states.

Most historians hail the Northwest Ordinance because of its anti-slavery provision. What they fail to say, which is typical of the hypocrisy and/or ignorance of white America's educators and scholarship, is that its anti-slavery provision was meant to protect the interests of the Southern slave owners. It was not, as historians are wont to imply, an indication that white America was morally opposed to slavery in a way that mattered. Certainly, slavery was wrong; they knew that and wanted it to not exist. But were they willing to sacrifice any of their profits in order to correct that wrong? Not at all, and that is the bottom line statement. Like Thomas Jefferson, their morality on the issue of slavery was worthless when it needed to matter most.

The Northwest Territory eventually added 5 states to the United States of America; Ohio, Indiana, Illinois, Michigan and Wisconsin. The original 13 colonies had now become an imperial power, and all of their conquests were at the expense of the Native American populations. Like Cristobal Colon, white America was ruthless when dealing with people who were militarily weaker and, like Colon, white America was lucky. At about the time that George Washington was taking the oath of office for the first time, events were taking place in the Caribbean that were completely beyond the control of the United States. Yet, these developments would result in the acquisition of the Louisiana Territory and spread the United States empire far west of the Mississippi River.

By 1800 Napoleon Bonaparte, the Corsican military genius, had envisioned a French empire in the Americas that included all of the area between the Mississippi River and the Rocky Mountains. Napoleon's American empire hinged on the French colony of San Domingo, which was so prosperous that the British tried to cripple it by declaring the worldwide abolition of the African slave trade. The Louisiana Territory, the name given to the lands between the Mississippi River and the Rocky Mountains, was possessed by the Spanish. Early American history maps listed the territory as Spanish owned, but the Spanish recognized that they did not own most of that territory. In fact, Spain's own maps of the Louisiana Territory listed the names of the Native Americans ("Indians") who actually owned the land. One of the prominent names of Native Americans listed is that of the Washitaw, Black "Indians" who had travelled to this land from Africa, settled here long before the Red "Indians" arrived and established a settled social order and lifestyle that reflected that of their African ancestors. The Washitaw, like many Native American people, were not nomads who lived in tepees. They lived in agriculture based communities whose economy was supplemented by fishing and hunting activities. [We will discuss the Washitaw more later in this chapter.]

By way of a secret treaty in October, 1800, Spain turned over its claim to the Louisiana Territory to Napoleon Bonaparte, who kept the treaty secret for nearly 15 months in order to maneuver himself into the best position possible. Napoleon knew that halting the rebellion in the colony of San Domingo was the first step in the development of his new American empire. Once it was quelled (he intended to kill all of the Black slaves who were there and replace them with new slaves from Africa), he could more confidently proclaim his new empire, assert its legitimacy and give it the military backing it would require.

As I made clear 25 years ago in <u>Ten Lessons: An Introduction to Black History</u>, the rebellion in San Domingo was not to be quelled. The former slaves of San Domingo committed themselves to fight for freedom or die in the process and, under the leadership of Toussaint L'Ouverture, destroyed the French military forces and proclaimed their independence. This defeat of Napoleon by the Blacks of San Domingo, now called Haiti, destroyed Napoleon's plans for an American empire and prompted him out of desperation to sell his claims in the Louisiana Territory to the United States. This doubled the size of the country and eventually added 13 more states to the union (Louisiana, Arkansas, Missouri, Iowa, Minnesota, North Dakota, South Dakota, Nebraska, Kansas, Oklahoma, Colorado, Wyoming and Montana).

Anyone who reads any history of the United States learns that this transaction was low down and steeped in controversy from the very beginning. Even white American historians freely point out the illegitimacy of the purchase and developments subsequent to it. As was just stated, Spain's own maps and many of France's recognized that the land Napoleon was selling to the United States, with the exception of New Orleans, was not owned by Spain and was not included in the secret treaty of 1800 that transferred ownership from Spain to France. Spanish and French maps recognized that all of the land beyond New Orleans had no white settlers and was owned by Black and Red Native Americans, most notably the Washitaw. Then president Thomas Jefferson knew this; that is why, prior to Napoleon's defeat at the hands of the Blacks of San Domingo, Jefferson offered Napoleon

$10 million for New Orleans and Florida (7 1/2 million dollars for New Orleans alone). Jefferson knew that if Napoleon accepted the offer, the French presence in America and military threat to the United States would be totally eliminated. Jefferson knew precisely what Napoleon actually owned, and that precise knowledge guided him in making his initial offer to Napoleon.

But Jefferson and Napoleon were alike; both knew how to ignore the facts when it was to his advantage to do so. Napoleon knew he did not own the Louisiana Territory, but he would easily ignore that fact if someone was willing to pay him for it because it would provide some badly needed money to the French treasury. And Jefferson knew that Napoleon did not own the Louisiana Territory, but he was willing to ignore that fact and buy it from Napoleon because it would give the United States the excuse it needed to claim ownership of 828,000 square miles of land that the United States had no legal right to. For less than $13 million total, it was a steal!

In April of 1803, the deal was completed. It was not only the grandest of thefts, but also unconstitutional according to French and American laws and a breach of the secret treaty of 1800 between France and Spain. According to the French constitution, no French territory could be sold without a meeting of the French legislature. No meeting of the French legislature took place. According to the American constitution, the United States president could not acquire land by treaty or promise statehood to people who were settled in a territory. Jefferson's purchase of Louisiana breached both provisions. And, as a term of the treaty between Napoleon and Spain, France promised to not sell Louisiana to another country. Needless to say, France did.

But people who are accustomed to power realities realize that treaties and laws are merely words on paper; to be strictly adhered to only by those who are too weak or too meek to take a definitive stand. The rightful owners of the land were far too weak, the Black People of Washitaw included.

Like all of the Native Americans, the Washitaw never established land and territorial boundaries in the manner that was unique to white people. In North America, the area from the Allegheny Mountains west to the Rocky Mountains, from Canada south to the Gulf of Mexico, including Florida, and West beyond the Rockies was recognized as Washitaw territory. This was more than 30 million acres of land. Long before the arrival of white settlers, a network of extensive trading posts across the land that reminded one of Africa existed and thrived, prompting Abraham Lincoln to later refer to it as "the Egypt of the West." Though the Washitaw were not able to defend the vast Louisiana Territory, they were literate and sophisticated enough to file legal papers in U.S. and European courts before Napoleon could effect his proposed sale. In so doing, they made their ownership of the Louisiana Territory beyond contradiction, and can point to treaties, maps, conventions, Supreme Court cases and other legal documents that prove their claims. In 1805, in response to the claims filed by the Washitaw, the American ministers in the court of Spain proposed that a neutral strip thirty leagues wide (approximately 90 miles) that would separate the U.S. lands from the Spanish territories be declared Washitaw territory. This 30 league wide strip would extend north and south along the entire length of the Mississippi River. Needless to say, this proposal went the way of all of the proposals and treaties that white people designed to recognize and protect the rights of Native American peoples.

Louisiana land records reaffirmed the fact that Washitaw land was never ceded to the United States and was never a part of the state of Louisiana. Additionally, on June 30, 1834, Congress declared that the parts of the United States that were west of the Mississippi River and not within the states of Missouri and Louisiana or the territory of Arkansas would be "Indian" country, and that no white person would be allowed to settle there. In spite of affirmations like that, the case of the Washitaw lingered. After several years of litigation, attempts were made to have the matter resolved in the U.S. Supreme Court, which, on June 19th, 1848, decided that only the laws of Spain held jurisdiction over contracts originated by the Spanish government. This was an indirect admission that the claims of the Washitaw were legitimate, and an indirect admission that the United States government had gone into a fraudulent arrangement with France that resulted in the theft of 828,000 square miles of land from the Black "Indians" who called themselves Washitaw. It was also a clear indication that the United States had no intention of returning that property to its rightful owners.

IV. Native American Policy

In the Introduction to <u>Bury My Heart At Wounded Knee</u>, Dee Brown, the author, deliberately referred to the "opening" of the American West. Brown, I assume, was trying to bring the readers' attention to the deceitful and misleading nature of that term. In fact, the west was not "opened", it was being ridded of what remained of its native inhabitants. America's legitimate West was being exterminated and ruthlessly replaced with militaristic, business centric, non-American foreigners.

The process started on October 12, 1492, when Cristobal Colon, not knowing where he was, tripped across the land mass of San Salvador. Colon and his Spanish crew, in search of fame and riches, quickly recognized the humane nature and non-militaristic make-up of Native American inhabitants and their institutions, and immediately began a process that revolved around their enslavement, decimation and extermination. Colon's major objective was to collect riches for himself, the Spanish crown and the members of his crew. It did not matter to him or any other white person that their prosperity would come at the expense of impoverishing and exterminating Native American families and communities.

In the early 1600s, English speaking white people landed in Virginia and Massachusetts. The conduct of the whites immediately threatened the institutions, lifestyles and very existence of the Native Americans who occupied those areas. As white businesses and individuals realized how much land they could grab and how wealthy they could become, they organized an assault against the Native Americans that was so disrespectful, audacious and genocidal that the Native Americans were forced to try to defend themselves to avoid extinction. Their efforts were doomed to failure, however. I have explained why previously, in my book <u>Ten Lessons: An Introduction to Black History</u>.

From the 1600s through the 1800s, the white assault against Native Americans continued and intensified. The assault took several forms, most of them characteristically cowardly. White people massacred Native American villages that were occupied only by women and children. White people massacred entire villages while the Native Americans slept. White people sneakily poisoned the food and water supplies of Native Americans, and tried to eliminate key elements of the Native Americans' survival construct (e.g., killing off the buffalo). White people entered into legal agreements with Native Americans that Native Americans had no understanding of, and made land transfer treaties with Native Americans that were immoral and ethically disgusting. White people infected blankets and clothes with deadly diseases that were unknown to Native Americans and, as acts of "good will," donated those infected items to unsuspecting Native Americans. White people systematically ignored laws that were designed to protect Native Americans and repeatedly uprooted and relocated Native American families as if they were herds of horses, goats and cows. Most of the scalping activities were carried out by white Americans against Native Americans, and white Americans typically beheaded Native American leaders and left their skulls on public display. Many of the early white heroes made their reputation by using high powered rifles and guns to fight against Native Americans who had bows and arrows. And if a Native American should defend his dignity and honor, insist on his humanity or retaliate after being attacked by a white invader, white Americans would intensify their genocidal measures against Native Americans, enact stiffer laws to legitimize their abuse of Native Americans and use their means of propaganda and education to popularize their assertion that Native Americans were uncivilized culprits and the cause and source of their own demise and misery.

So that men in high and low places might make a profit and get rich and powerful, the Native Americans were deprived of their land, treated with the greatest amount of disrespect and scorn, and practically exterminated. Andrew Jackson, the eighth President of the United States, is a prime example of this. Andrew Jackson was a 21 year old lawyer in Cumberland County, Tennessee in 1788. According to white records, Cumberland County had been "purchased" from the Cherokees in 1785. Records of this purchase are undoubtedly fraudulent because Native Americans did not have the same concept of land ownership as white people did, so it was impossible for them to sell land. Because Native Americans did not understand English or generate written records, it is certain that their understanding of what they agreed to with the whites of Cumberland County was entirely different from what the whites claim they agreed to. In any regard, Andrew Jackson was elected to the U.S. Senate in 1797, left the Senate for financial reasons (he wasn't getting rich quickly enough) and became major general of the Tennessee militia.

It was the militia that proved to be the key to Andrew Jackson's quest for riches and power. He achieved national prominence by attacking Native American villages, forcing them to give up land and removing them to reservations. Andrew Jackson and his cohorts frequently attained the titles to much of the land they forced the Native Americans to give up. As a result, by the time he died, Andrew Jackson had not only become a powerful man, he was an extremely rich man. He had been elected President of the United States, owned several estates, hundreds of heads of horses, cows, and other livestock, hundreds of slaves and more than 3000 acres of land that had once belonged to America's original modern inhabitants.

It was the intention of white people throughout the American states to do exactly what Andrew Jackson was to do. They wanted land, they wanted riches, and they wanted power. In the Native Americans, they saw the key to each of their goals. By stealing the land from the Native Americans, they could open the path to riches, and by bloodily removing the Native American from the American landscape, they could gain fame and power.

In a nutshell, this quest for fame, fortune and power, coupled with white people's belief in the white mythology (their "superiority" and right to prosper at the expense of other people's blood, sweat and tears), was the motivating factor in the virtual extermination of Native American peoples. From Jamestown to Plymouth Rock, one finds the legacy of this reality. From Rhode Island to Vermont, New Hampshire and Maine, from Manhattan to Niagara Falls, from Georgia to Alabama and Mississippi, from Virginia to Kentucky, Indiana and Illinois, from Louisiana to Oklahoma and Montana; the process went on and on and on. The land and riches of Native Americans became the land and riches of white invaders, and Native American populations disappeared, to be replaced by white populations. Only after the sustained and systematic massacre of Native Americans had been completed did white Americans with a "conscience" endeavor to listen to the Native Americans' side of the story. Only after the souls and institutions of Native Americans had been practically erased from their hearts and memories did "objective" white Americans give them credit for their high level of civilization. Only after the Native Americans had been made all but extinct did white Americans with a "sense of justice" admit to the Native Americans' humanity and rights. But the white "conscience," "objectivity" and "sense of justice" were the typical little white American choo choos that do not matter at all. White

Americans did not attempt to return what they had stolen or atone for the wrongs they had committed against Native Americans. White Americans did, however, establish Native American monuments, name states, cities, cars and boats after Native American tribes, and place pictures of Native Americans shedding a tear on trash cans and billboards. To expect anything of more substance is to not understand the white power forces that drive and dominate the United Sates of America.

The expansion westward was completed at the expense of a militarily inept and politically perturbed Mexico. The westward lands that were not included in the Louisiana Territory were generally accepted as Mexican territory, but the Mexican government was proving itself incapable of maintaining or defending it. In the 1820s, Mexico made the grave mistake of recognizing the right of Stephen F. Austin, a white American, to settle American families in Texas. Within a decade, the American settlers had seceded from Mexico and were seeking entry into the United States. Because politicians in the United States were divided on the issue, annexation stalled and Texas declared itself an independent nation. This opened the possibility that Texas might abolish slavery, which might have become a nightmare for Southerners if their slaves had begun to flee to Texas and freedom. John Tyler, U. S. President and slave owning Virginian, sidestepped the opposition by recommending Texas be admitted by a joint resolution of Congress. This was not constitutional but it was done, and Texas quickly became the 28th state.

To obtain New Mexico, Arizona and California, President James Polk baited Mexico into a war. The Treaty of Guadeloupe Hidalgo officially ended the hostilities in 1848 and ceded not only the states listed above, but Texas as well. That might well have been an admission that Texas' earlier admission to the union was the consequence of fraudulent proceedings. Be that as it may, the territories of the continental United States now extended from the Atlantic to the Pacific, and the slogan "manifest destiny" had been converted into a political reality.

V. Unpaid and Underpaid Labor

The quickest way to get rich is to not pay the people who work for you. That practice was applied by Cristobal Colon, with rewarding consequences for the Spanish and devastating consequences for Native Americans. It was also applied by the Englishmen who landed at Jamestown and Plymouth Rock and their descendants, and the consequences were just as rewarding for the Englishmen and just as devastating for the Red and Black Native Americans and Africans who did the work.

White people who came to America literally impoverished Native Americans and Africans and worked them to death. The fact that Native American and African laborers were not fairly compensated constitutes one of the greatest financial thefts and acts of economic genocide in the history of humankind. Because the wealth of Africans and Native Americans was legally but immorally and unethically transferred from its legitimate owners to a collection of politically empowered thieves, a system of haves and have nots prevailed that makes a mockery of the popular rhetoric of the United States to this day. Many of the ills of American society can be traced to this huge imbalance between the haves and the have nots. Those who have wealth and use it intelligently can acquire power; those who don't have wealth can not. Those who have wealth can produce valuable commodities; those who don't have wealth can not. Those who have wealth can fail to perform if they don't get fair returns for their services; those who don't have wealth can not. Those who have wealth can purchase the goods, services and commodities that improve the quality of life; those who don't have wealth can not. Those who have wealth can adequately feed, clothe, educate, house and provide medical care for themselves; those who don't have wealth can not. Those who have wealth can retard the onslaught of poverty and all that poverty implies; those who don't

have wealth can not. Those who have wealth can generate more wealth, accumulate more power and better
develop the ability to protect and defend themselves;
those who don't have wealth can not. Thus, white America
did not just take money from the Native Americans and
Africans when it robbed them of their labor, it took away
their ability to develop properly and stripped them of the
energy they needed to exploit their human potential.

I can not overemphasize the fact that the exploitation and abuse of Native American and African labor WAS
LEGAL! White American representatives and institutions
have put so much emphasis on respecting and abiding
by the law that its citizens tend to forget that there is
nothing inherently fair or just about the laws humans are
apt to enact. In spite of all the propaganda to the contrary, individuals have to remember that the laws that
should be respected and abided by the most are nature's
laws. When what is legal according to certain human beings is not in line with what our consciences tell us is
correct, we have to be fair minded and just enough to
ignore man made laws and observe those of a higher
order. If enough individuals were upright enough to do
that, the majority of the most heinous crimes ever committed against humans and humankind would never have
taken place, and much of the undue suffering human
beings have experienced would have been precluded as
well.

Robbing people of the just rewards of their labor has
been one of white America's trademarks. While Native
Americans and Africans have borne the brunt of this theft,
they have not been the only ones. In the 1820s, white
immigrants from Europe were brought over to help in the
construction of canals and railways. These whites, not
the descendants of white America's early settlers, were
looked down on and denied easy access to "the pursuit
of happiness," but because they came over by the hundreds of thousands, their political potential was recognized and exploited by American forces that were not
quite acceptable to the powers that were. As a result,

they were encouraged to become politically active and formed the nucleus of several labor unions. Not long afterwards, they were involved in organized work stoppages, forcing concessions from their employers and bringing a measure of respect to the everyday white worker. Later, after the Civil War period, Chinese, Filipino and other Oriental people were imported so they could work for unfair wages. Since Oriental workers were not white, they were not imported in large numbers, not readily recruited into political parties and labor unions and unable to gain the respect European worker immigrants had managed to gain. White America recognized no limits as it ruthlessly exploited Oriental workers, and the prosperity white America realized as a consequence can not be accurately tabulated.

White America's rationale for using unpaid and underpaid labor is cited repeatedly in books written by traditional historians: the whites had to choose between some form of forced labor and poverty. That is certainly not the case. What the whites had to choose between was distributing the wealth generated by labor equitably or inequitably. In its typically self-serving manner, white America chose the latter. By so doing, it continued a white American tradition, a tradition that is held in high esteem even to this day.

Not paying and underpaying laborers is a criminal activity, and white America knows that. However, it is typical of white America to commit an act that it knows is a crime, create a mythology to rationalize the criminal act, and then rid the act of its criminal essence by legalizing it. Black and Red Native Americans were forced to work for free and practically exterminated. White America knew these were criminal acts, but rather than stop committing those crimes, white America created the myth of the "bad injun" who attacked innocent white settlers and made killing them a legitimate activity. White America knew it was criminal to enslave Black People, but rather than stop doing so, they created the myth of the Black savage and declared that slavery was their natural state.

Popularizing a mythology and legalizing the criminal are critical when one's objective is to de-prioritize justice. White America, historically, has been quite efficient at de-prioritizing justice when it is to white America's financial advantage to do so. Students of American history can't afford to turn a deaf ear or blind eye to that reality.

VI. Sectional Hostilities

The white Englishmen who settled the new land could not get along with each other. Rather than rally around a national picture, they remained strapped inside local and regional snapshots that rendered them incapable of magnifying their likenesses, acting in the interest of the whole and resolving their differences in a civilized manner. Because they were so incapable, the Civil War seemed inevitable, and the Civil War was fought.

From day one, it seemed that a war among English settlers in America was inevitable. As colonies, they probably would have been shooting each other as a matter of policy if it had not been for the presence of Great Britain. Later, as a condition of forming a new union, they agreed to a federal constitution that centered on strong states rights and a weak central government because they did not trust each other. With the formation of the union, the state governments ceded their territories to the federal government on the provision that the federal government swiftly rid those territories of Native Americans and open them to new settlers. When the federal government proved incapable of moving as quickly as it had promised, recognized leaders in some of the states went into a political frenzy, threatened to renege on their membership in the union and called for secession.

Secession. How often that word was heard during the first 80 years of the country's existence. Thoughts of secession and nullifying the union seemed to come from everywhere. Mountain men from Pennsylvania, upset by a tax on rum, started a Whiskey Rebellion and threatened to secede, while poor farmers in every state, particularly Massachusetts and North Carolina, rebelled and resolved to govern themselves because the political establishment represented men of property and offered no financial relief or promise for others. In the West, which at the time was east of the Mississippi River, the settlers wanted the United States to guarantee shipping access to the Mississippi River. If this guarantee could not be delivered, its political and economic leaders felt it would be in their best interest to secede from the union and establish political ties with France. Additionally, land speculators and settlers who had made plans to capitalize on the spread of the plantation system westward were infuriated by new American tariffs that drove up the cost of British goods. They often talked of secession, as did Southerners who felt that tariffs enacted by the federal government always favored the North at the expense of the South. Missouri's petition for statehood nearly tore the country apart. That was saved by the Missouri Compromise, which itself became the source of secessionist talk 30 years later. After Texas became an independent republic in the 1840s, many politicians in the South thought it might be to their advantage to secede from the United States and become a part of Texas. In the 1850s alone, the Dred Scott decision, the mad rush for Kansas and the African slave trade all resulted in talks of a breakup of the union. Even the Wisconsin legislature was attempting to void federal laws. And, there was the perennial issue of fundamentally different labor systems that propelled dissimilar types of capitalist development and expansion. They could not co-exist as part of the same entity. The only question was, "How would they go about their separate ways?"

To avoid secession, varying states at varying times argued that they had the right to nullify any federal law or declare it unconstitutional within their borders. Although not formally espoused until 1828, nullification had been an issue from the day the new republic was borne. As early as the 1790s, Georgia had effectively nullified a Supreme Court decision that required the state to repay certain war debts. Georgia's action held the day because it was supported by all of the states, and eventually resulted in the passage of Article 11 of the U. S. Constitution. However, it was a rare occasion when a large number of states would benefit from the same complaint. As a result, most of the states were normally opposed to nullification initiatives.

In the 1830s, South Carolina took nullification to its extreme. Upset by what it perceived as a series of unfair tariffs, South Carolina's state legislature declared that the tariffs imposed by the federal act of 1828 were null and void within the state, forbade federal officials to collect such taxes within the state and threatened to secede if the federal government attempted to force the state to comply. South Carolina raised a volunteer force to protect the state against federal intrusion, and Andrew Jackson prepared to use the federal army and navy to collect the required tariffs. To avoid bloodshed and allow both parties a way out, Congress proposed to lower the tariffs. South Carolina's legislature responded by repealing the nullification directive. Though South Carolina had not succeeded in nullifying a federal law or leaving the union, it had proved that a single state could threaten the union and force the federal government to take extraordinary measures. What could a collection of states do?

It is noteworthy that Andrew Jackson called the tariff a "pretext" used by South Carolina to test nullification and secession. Jackson added that the next pretext would be "the Negro, or slavery question." Jackson's statements both anticipated the Civil War and exposed its real cause. Jackson knew that the Civil War would not be fought for morality reasons or to free the slaves, it would be fought because of sectional incompatibilities that only a war could resolve. The Civil War would be fought by Southerners to free the South and by Northerners to free the North. More specifically, it would be fought by Southerners to free Southern capitalism, which depended on slavery, and by Northerners and Westerners to free Northern capitalism, which was intent on dominating the entire country. If history had been concerned about clarity, the Civil War would have been fought during the early 1830s, at the time of the tariff controversy. However, the other Southern states did not feel the pinch of the tariff as severely as South Carolina, and failed to come to South Carolina's defense. That allowed nearly 30 additional years of moral posturing and political propaganda to obscure the issue and convince otherwise intelligent individuals that the Civil War revolved around a moral issue and the conscience of a nation. Nothing could be farther from the truth.

Chapter 22:
War In America

I. White America Attacks Black People

"Another method of punishment... is to dig a hole in the ground large enough for the slave to squat or lay down in. The victim is then stripped naked and placed in the hole, and a covering or grafting of green sticks is laid over the opening. Upon this a quick fire is built, and the live embers sifted through upon the naked flesh of the slave, until his body is blistered and swollen almost to bursting. With just enough of life to enable him to crawl, the slave is then allowed to recover from his wounds if he can, or to end his suffering by death." <u>The Black Book</u> p. 9

I have already summed up the systematic attack made by white America against Black and Red Native Americans. Now I will give a similar summary of white America's attacks on the Black Africans who were brought to this land as slaves, and summarize the African's response to these attacks.

In the same way white Americans dehumanized Native Americans, white Americans dehumanized the Blacks who were brought or came to the United States. African men, women and children were classified as chattel, which put them on the same level as cattle and horses, and no Black individuals had a right that white individuals or white laws were obligated to recognize. Blacks on the slave auction block were inspected in the most dehumanizing ways, and in no small degree to satisfy the weird sexual curiosity of their prospective owners. Blacks were confined to sleeping quarters that were not fit for pigs, with no heat to warm them in the winter and nothing but hard earth to serve as a bed. The food Blacks were forced to eat did not even have a nutritious pretense; it was the worst their "owners" could provide them with without rendering them incapable of performing hard work. Medical care for Blacks was a non-consideration, along with any feelings of humanity, particularly when whites felt push had come to shove. White America tried to convince itself that Black People were not people at all. Black People were tools, resources, assets, liabilities, property with motor abilities that, like dogs and donkeys, happened to inhale, exhale and perform all of the functions that animals regularly perform. Black People were items that could be exchanged for a keg of rum, mounted when the master felt horny or mated to produce additional "wenches" and "bucks." But more than anything else, as far as the white psyche was concerned, Black People were the key to economic prosperity and a status symbol. Astute Southerners were quick to point out that a cotton plantation was the best thing a capitalist could invest in, but the cost of slaves was getting so high that the average southerner, alas, soon might not be able to afford one.

Black People made white individuals rich and famous and highly regarded institutions like Brown University possible, and it wasn't just because of cotton. Black People made it possible for not only cotton to become a money crop in the United States, but tobacco, rice, indigo and others as well; and enabled several industries to emerge that otherwise would not have done so in like manner. Because of Black People, the cities where white people who had been made rich lived and congregated evolved into centers of American living and culture.

Black People not only provided physical labor for the benefit of white people, but were craftsmen and excelled at every major occupation, both skilled and unskilled. Black People did white people's mining work, built white people's churches, cathedrals and other socially significant structures, cooked, washed and pressed white people's clothes, raised white people's children, functioned as white people's nurses and midwives, built and cleaned white people's homes, did artwork on white people's buildings, composed and played music for white people in orchestras and on plantations, made white people's shoes and provided white people with satisfying entertainment. Indeed, Black People provided white people throughout America with an income and a lifestyle.

To demonstrate this, let's look at the slave trade. The slave trade was a lucrative business. Usually a person made a 30% to 40% net profit on every slave sold. The slave trade was not only profitable as a trading activity, it gave rise to untold numbers of other industries that gave employment to white Americans. Millions of white people were needed to build ships, to make and transport guns, to make ammunition, to manufacture, smelt and sell iron, to build boats, to paint ships, homes and other structures, to make the hundreds of items that were used to bribe dim-witted Africans in Africa, etc. It is true! The Black People who were transported to America from Africa provided the economic support for hundreds of thousands of small white families (4 or 5 persons each) throughout Europe and the Americas. And, incredibly, that is only part of the story.

The Industrial Revolution, which changed the quality of life in the white world, would have been a different process without the monies generated by the slave trade and slave labor. Indeed, modern industry in the white world was made possible as a result of the slave trade and slavery (the abuse of Black People). The blood, sweat and tears of enslaved Black People financed the Industrial Revolution and catapulted New York and the United States to the forefront of the capitalist world. Those are facts that no objective historian would deny.

What, then, was white America's reaction to Black People? In a word, psychopathic. White people enjoyed the fact that Black People were making them rich, and they enjoyed the fact that they could point to the condition of Black People to prove that Black People deserved to be slaves and white people were a superior people. However, white people detested Black People because the presence of Black People constantly reminded them of the grave criminal act they were committing, and Black People's ability to adapt and thrive in spite of the ruthless conditions imposed by whites convinced white people that, if a superior human existed, it was certainly not wrapped in a pale, colorless skin. This contradiction was the source of grave conflicts for white people. Whites knew that the white reality and the highly promoted white mythology, all too often, were diametrically in disaccord with each other, and that the Black reality, all too often, was diametrically opposed to the image of Black People popularized and promulgated by white people.

The conflict between what they wanted to be true and what they knew was true helped prompt white people to try to erase that part of reality that conflicted with their mythology. A major part of this erasure campaign evidenced itself in attacks on Black People. From day one, white institutions and individuals viciously attacked Black People. Their intent was to eradicate the truth that belied their claims, and to simultaneously destroy every Black person who came to this land; while at the same time continuing to rely on Black People for a steady and permanent source of free labor.

It has been said that the perpetrator of a crime never forgives his victims. White people never forgave the Native Americans, and they never forgave the Africans who were brought to this country as slaves. The worst characteristics of white people emerged when they were in the presence of Black People, and the results were devastating. White people roasted Blacks rotisserie style, beat Blacks with a psychotic vengeance, systematically separated Black families and destroyed whatever sense of familyhood Blacks might have had, chopped open the wombs of pregnant Black women, knifed and axed off Black ears, fingers, hands and penises, rammed sticks up Black rear ends, hanged Black necks, branded a variety of Black body parts, raped Black girls and women and sicced the dogs on whatever Blacks tried to escape their venom. Black males and females were incarcerated without just cause, convicted of crimes they did not commit, and wrongfully executed by white individuals and white governments as a matter of course. Black People were

legally robbed, denied adequate judicial redress and terrorized when they complained. Whites made it illegal for
Blacks to be educated or learn how to read, illegal for
Blacks to congregate without the permission or presence
of a white person, illegal for Blacks to seek political power
and undesirable for Blacks to adequately feed and clothe
themselves or compete with white individuals. Thus, white
people made it nearly impossible for Black children to
develop into responsible Black adults, and for Black adults
to raise children in a manner that was to the child's and
Black People's benefit. White America, in the midst of
reaping the benefits of Black labor, declared war on the
Black People who provided them with incomes, status
and high standards of living and waged that war relent-
lessly, unceasingly. Almost from day one, then, there was
undeclared war in America, that war was waged by white
people against Black People and that war continues to
this day.

II. Black People Defend Themselves

"She said, that when the officers and slave-hunters
came to the house in which they were concealed, she
caught a shovel and struck two of the children on the
head, and then took a knife and cut the throat of the
third, and tried to kill the other,-- that if they had given
her time, she would have killed them all-- that with regard to herself, she cared but little; but she was unwilling
to have her children suffer as she had done.
"I inquired if she was not excited to madness when
she committed the act. No, she replied, I was as cool as
I am now; and would much rather kill them at once, and
thus end their sufferings, than have them taken back to
slavery, and be murdered by piece-meal." The Black Book

"A negro has been tarred and feathered, by his col-
ored brethren... in consequence of it being cleared [sic]
proved that he was in the employ of slaveholders..." The
Black Book

"You only do to me what the British would have done to George Washington had they caught him." Gabriel Prosser

White America declared war on Black People, but unlike Native Americans, Blacks had had enough experience to withstand the attacks and fight white America back. The Africans who were brought to America as slaves had been fighting against Arabic invaders for more than a thousand years, and had had encounters with other European adventurers before coming into contact with the Spanish, English and their descendants. They were not totally prepared for the brutality and persistence of white America's attacks, but unlike Native Americans, they were not totally unprepared for it. They had a basis for competing against it, a proven metaphysical resistance, that enabled them to hold on and multiply under circumstances that would have caused others to wither and die out.

Fighting back was difficult and painful for Blacks in America, and not as effective as it should have been. To begin with, the slaves were all too frequently too civilized to seek "an eye for an eye" or "a tooth for a tooth." As civilized people are wont to do, the slaves fought with the hope that their attackers would come to recognize the wrongness of their ways and change. As a consequence, Blacks took on a disproportionately large burden of the suffering that was caused by this war and a disproportionately small share of the good that came out of it. As unfair as that may sound, that is what usually happens when people who fight a war care too much about the elevation of their enemies and not enough about the elevation of themselves. War is not a socially redeeming process; not the activity of people who are driven by civilized inclinations. The nature of war is to dismantle and devastate your enemy; socially, economically, psychologically, politically and otherwise. Those who fail to attempt to do this, those who fail to recognize the complete barbarity of war and fail to conduct war accordingly, strip it of its essential nature, decrease its probability of helping them or bettering their lot and, unwittingly, set themselves up as the disproportionate recipients of its wrath.

To compound the mistake of trying to conduct a civilized war, the effectiveness of the Black response to being attacked by whites was hampered by the fact that they came from so many rival cultures. Instead of mounting effective and sustained offensives against their abusers, they fought as disunited people; haphazardly, inefficiently, without the necessary level of confidence in fellow Blacks and without the required level of co-ordination. In short, they failed to harness their rebellious energy appropriately and, quite predictably, did not benefit from the release of that energy nearly as much as they should have.

The majority of the Blacks were rebellers, but they were not effective rebellers. Spitting in white people's cup was a popular form of resistance, but it was not a threat to the institution of slavery. The same can be said of "breaking the hoe" and similar acts of subversion. Putting poison in the master's food was a stronger form of resistance and resulted in the elimination of several whites, but it too was not a threat to the institution of slavery (it was never done on a large enough scale). In order to effectively communicate with white people, Black People would have to daringly and continually speak the language white people understood. That language had little or nothing to do with words. Actions were what caught white people's attention, and some actions meant more than others.

The resistance activities of the Underground Railroad caught white people's attention. However, the Underground Railroad was more a nuisance than anything else because white people quickly realized that it would never be an effective threat to the institution of slavery. The North was not "free" territory and slaves were not running away from the plantations in large numbers, so serious limitations were placed on what the Underground Railroad could accomplish. What the Underground Railroad did was to rid certain slaveowners of some their property, some of their assets, or something they had paid for. As such, the Underground Railroad was a threat to the bottom financial line of certain planters, but it was not a threat to the institution of slavery.

The Blacks who preferred death to slavery were made of the right stuff. However, when in a state of war, simply being made of the right stuff is not enough. It was incumbent that the Blacks register their disaccord with slavery in the most effective manner. It was not enough to sidestep slavery by taking your life or the life of some loved ones. What was called for was an ongoing attack on the system of slavery, its practitioners and its supporters. If the Blacks were willing to put their life on the line, they should have done so in combat against their enemies. Killing oneself or one's loved ones in order to avoid the life of a slave is the bravest of acts, but it served no essential anti-slavery purpose. It did not send the right message to other Blacks, and it did not send the right message to the whites who were victimizing Blacks.

Prior to the Civil War, four possible anti-slavery scenarios sent the right message to white people in the right way. One of these scenarios was that of runaway slaves who formed maroon communities. A second of these scenarios was that of rebellious slaves who plotted to destroy slavery and establish independent, self-governing Black states. The third of these scenarios was the existence of a "free" country that bordered on the Southern states. And the fourth of these scenarios was the mass migration of slaves away from the plantations. White people recognized that either of these activities could have undone slavery, but white people in all parts of the country were against the first two because they not only threatened the institution of slavery, they threatened the reign of white power in America.

A white life was cheap as far as maroons and Black rebellers were concerned. White people were well aware of that, and the mere thought of Black rebellers and maroons sent shivers of fear throughout their bodies. But, the whites who thought in more fundamental terms realized that the maroons were not powerful enough to undo the institution of slavery. The threat posed by the maroons was more indirect than direct; it kept an alternative to slavery constantly in front of each and every Black person. All a slave had to do was build up enough nerve and "want to" to run away and live the life of a fugitive.

The maroons were a headache to white people, make no mistake about that. They frequently lived off of goods that were taken from neighboring plantations, but they did not have the assets needed to pose a military threat to white power. Additionally, every Black slave knew that a Black person could be "free;" there were a handful of freed Blacks in every locale. Why experience "freedom" as a fugitive when there was a distant but somewhat realistic alternative? Every slave could dream of the prospect of a freedom that did not require the level of insecurity and privation that the maroons had to endure. With a little bit of luck, a slave could buy his/her freedom, be granted freedom by a master or go North via the Underground Railroad. Options such as these that could be imagined by each and every slave reduced the allure of becoming a maroon, and reduced the ability of the maroons to impact on the institution of slavery.

White people viewed maroon activities and slave rebellions in quite different perspectives. Whites knew that an effective slave rebellion could completely disrupt the institution of slavery, and needed look no further than Haiti to be reminded of that fact. Whites also knew that there were plenty of Blacks who were able and willing to participate in slave rebellions. They knew of slave rebellions that took place on the trip across the Atlantic, and they knew of slave rebellions that took place after the ships had reached dock. For the 200 year period between 1650 and 1850, as many as 10,000 slave rebellions might have taken place in the United States alone, and possibly more. Every week, three or four times a month, Black individuals somewhere in the South were in the midst of planning a rebellion or carrying one out. How long would it be before the stars lined up in the favor of the Blacks? How long would it be before a rebellion took place that destroyed white Americans' willingness to take the risk that came with enslaving human beings? These are the questions that nagged each and every white individual.

The frequency of slave rebellions not only threatened the institution of slavery, it generated a high degree of psychological instability among white Southerners. Since the probability of a slave rebellion was so high, it took on a psychological warfare character, and tended to exact extreme white reactions. The mere rumor of a rebellion sent some whites into a fatalistic "the end has come" mode and others into a raging "kill all of the niggas" mode. As a matter of course, white people's intelligence seemed to somehow be short-circuited when it came to Black People. When a slave rebellion was believed imminent, there was not the slightest chance that logical thinking or objective responses would carry the day.

It was not lost on the whites that the Blacks who became maroons and rebellers wanted an independent government and country of their own. Fortunately for the whites, what the Blacks lacked then is what they lack now: the resolve and inclination to act en masse for the benefit of Blacks, regardless of the odds and its impact on non-Black groups of people. Additionally, during the time frame that this section covers, the defense the Blacks put up to repel the white attack was not as scientific, calculated and precise as it needed to be. This provided the whites with a huge advantage. Whereas the war waged by white America against Black People benefitted from a high level of organization, undaunted support and a clear objective, the resistance waged by Black People suffered from a low level of organization, a high level of tenuousness and the absence of a clear cut objective. In spite of all of those shortcomings, the Black maroons and rebellers could have undone the institution of slavery.

Could have, but didn't. The plans the rebellers laid out that could have made the necessary impact were often defeated by forces beyond their control. And in cases where enough of the uncontrollable factors were favorable to Black People, a Black individual would play the role of traitor and alert the whites to what was about to take place. But these type activities are a regular and normal part of war proceedings. Rarely do they defeat a determined people, rarely do they catapult an undeserving people to victory. They are simply part of a process; a process that, in this particular case, was weighted in favor of white power to such a huge extent that the immense blunders committed by the whites were still too small to undo them.

A bigger threat to slavery than even the slave rebellions was the policy of neighboring countries in regard to slavery. If the Northern states or any territory bordering on the South functioned as a "free" government, the institution of slavery would have been in trouble. White people's fear of free territory bordering on the South was borne out before the birth of the United States, when Georgia was settled for the expressed purpose of providing a buffer state between the South and Florida, a Spanish colony. In the 1840s, when Texas became an independent country, concern that Texas might outlaw slavery alarmed Southerners to no end and resulted in Texas being admitted to the Union under suspect circumstances. White Southerners knew that slaves would run to a neighboring country by the thousands every day if they knew they could enjoy protection against slave hunters once they got there.

After all was said and done, the fate of slavery laid in the hands of the slaves themselves. If they refused to be slaves, that would have settled the issue. They did not do this, however, until after the start of the War Between the States. At that time, the slaves began to vacate the South en masse. The result was immediate and definitive: the end of the institution of slavery, the triumph of Northern capitalism over Southern capitalism and victory for the North. But who could have imagined that this situation would ever have presented itself? Certainly not white people in any part of the United States, and certainly not the Black People in the South. An old antagonism, sectional incompatibilities, caused whites to become so emotionally embroiled in a family feud that an opportunity presented itself to the slaves that was totally out of character with everything else that was taking place. Thus, the least imaginable factor came into play and proved decisive. White people's tendency to commit blunders finally caught up with the institution of slavery. Whites left the South unguarded, and the Blacks took advantage of the blunder and freed themselves.

Black People freed themselves, but the war in America against Black People did not cease. Quite to the contrary, it increased in intensity. That issue will be discussed and dissected in the final chapters of this book.

Chapter 23:
The War Between the States

I. The Beginning of War

The North was not willing to take the step that would result in a war between the states. The South was not only willing, but eager.

The South, the home of slavery, took the step that led to the Civil War. If the South had not started that war in 1861, the war would not have been fought at that time. How, then, can it be argued that the war was fought to free the slaves? Indeed, the only freedom that interested the South was its freedom from the North.

Yet we hear it over and over, ever more forceful as more time passes: the Civil War was fought to free the slaves. That is proof that a mistruth repeated often enough takes on the prominence and potency of legitimacy, and that individuals and forces exist that systematically gain from the distortion of facts and the resulting ignorance of the people. How open and shut can a fact be? The South, the champions of slavery and the benefactors of a slave economy, started the War Between the States.

The way history has been written traditionally, and many of the events that took place can lead a student to the conclusion that the war was fought to free the slaves. But even as the events leading up to the Civil War seemed to revolve around slavery, slavery was not the issue. Slavery was the crutch the issue walked on, and it carried the weight so completely, so thoroughly, that it and the issue became indistinguishable in the eyes of many.

But few of the major players suffered from this blurring of factors. The major players in this development never lost sight of the sectional hostilities that had divided the country since day one. Those hostilities were the basis of a grand tug of war, a bitter family feud that increased in intensity and ignited so many primitive emotions that only a war could make purging them possible.

II. Pretexts and Crutches

As I stated earlier, in the 1830s Andrew Jackson called the tariff a "pretext" used by South Carolina to test nullification and secession. Jackson added that the next pretext would be "the Negro, or slavery question." Jackson was a major player and he knew; slavery would not be the issue that led to a war between the states, it would only serve as a pretext. The issue was economic freedom for the South versus economic freedom for the North. That was the only issue.

But confusion was rampant. Part of the confusion is due to the fact that there were minor players on the scene who were concerned about slavery and its implications for the nation as a whole. But these were minor players; they were incapable of making an issue so pressing that the country would split up and go to war to resolve it. But what they did was supply major players with fat that couldn't start a fire, but could appreciably increase its intensity.

From the days of the constitutional convention in Philadelphia, there was grave concern about maintaining a balance of power in Congress between the slave holding states and non-slave holding states. There was no moral element to this issue; it was totally economic and political. When Missouri applied for entrance as a slave state in 1819, this balance was threatened. The Missouri Compromise (1820) restored the balance by admitting Missouri and Maine (as a non-slave state), and establishing a legal model that could be followed to maintain the balance in the future.

In the 1850s, the debate over Kansas and Nebraska led to a proposal to undo the Missouri Compromise by allowing settlers of new territories to determine whether their state would be slave or non-slave. This gave slavery forces the impression that slavery was about to be suppressed, and gave anti-slavery forces the impression that slavery was about to be made legal throughout the country. Tempers reached the boiling point, and settlers flocked to Kansas to place their vote and spill the blood of their enemies. "Bleeding Kansas" made it clear to everyone that Civil War was no longer a question of if, but when. The battle over control of Kansas became a dry run for the battle over control of the country. In both cases, it seemed as if the dispute was driven by the issue of slavery. In both cases, that couldn't have been farther from the truth.

The confusion was multiplied when the Supreme Court issued the Dred Scott decision in 1857, and pro-slavery forces made calls to make the African slave trade legal again. Up to this point, the nation's rhetoric had claimed that freedom was national and slavery was sectional, but Chief Justice Roger Taney and the four other southern justices on the court flipped the rhetoric upside down by using the Dred Scott case to declare that the opposite was true; that slavery was national and freedom was sectional. The African slave trade, which was supposed to have ended in 1808, only became illegal on paper that year. It continued practically unmonitored by American forces until the beginning of the War Between the States. Southerners claimed that the political power of the North was being increased by white immigrant laborers, but the South could not increase its political power in like manner because the Black immigrant laborers the South needed were not legally allowed to enter the country.

Anti-slavery forces were alarmed by these two developments, and responded by declaring that the Fugitive Slave Act of 1850, which required Northerners to help in the recovery of runaway slaves, was unconstitutional. Then, the admission of Minnesota and Oregon into the Union as free states turned a one state advantage for the North into a three state advantage. The South could see the die being cast and, in a more schizophrenic state than ever, took note of the North's response to John Brown's raid on Harper's Ferry in 1859. When some Northerners showed admiration for John Brown's strike against slavery, the South was certain: Southerners would never be able to experience their way of life in peace as part of the United States of America.

In 1860 the die landed. Abraham Lincoln, an ideological opponent of slavery, was elected President of the United States. Being as schizophrenic as ever, the South did not care that, in spite of his opposition to slavery, Lincoln had no intention of ending it. The South wanted to be free. Within weeks (well before Lincoln could be inaugurated), seven Southern states had left the Union, formed the Confederate States of America and elected Jefferson Davis as its President. In the months that followed, four more states, including Virginia, would join them.

III. The War To Free The South

When the South seceded from the Union, the North made two attempts to save the Union by offering the South everything the South wanted. The first proposal, the Crittenden compromise, proposed six constitutional amendments that, among other things, forbade the abolition of slavery, guaranteed compensation to owners for runaway slaves, stretched "slave territory" to the Pacific Ocean and guaranteed that no future constitutional amendment could touch the issues of slavery, the 3/5 compromise or the fugitive slave law. This proposal clearly demonstrated that the North was not willing to go to war out of concern for the condition of the slaves, nor was the North concerned about freeing the slaves. But the South was not concerned about remaining a part of the Union, so this proposal got nowhere.

A second attempt, pushed on by more than 130 delegates from 21 states, suggested seven constitutional amendments, including a guarantee that neither Congress nor the country would EVER interfere with slavery in any state. Again, the North made it clear that it was not willing to go to war out of concern for the slaves, and was not concerned about freeing the slaves. Again, the South turned a deaf ear. How, then, can it be argued that the war was fought to free the slaves?

After seceding, the South took control of properties in the South that belonged to the Union government. The North was not willing to start a war to recover these properties! One of these properties, Fort Sumter, was still occupied by Union troops after Abraham Lincoln took office. Those troops, on the brink of running out of supplies, were prepared to surrender to Southern troops. The South, by allowing the Northern troops to surrender, could have gained control of Fort Sumter without firing a shot, and without starting a war. But that would have left the issue of Southern freedom up in the air. The South wanted to make a statement, to leave no room for doubt; it was a free and independent nation! The South, therefore, fired on Fort Sumter and started the war. The South, which had no intention of freeing the slaves, left the North no choice but to fight back or watch the Union dissolve. If the North let the Southern states secede, the remaining union states would get the impression that they could imitate the South and secede later on, if they chose to do so. That meant that the Union would be forever getting smaller and smaller, and less and less substantial. To keep that from happening, the North had to fight. The North had to fight, not to free the slaves, but to (1) preserve the old Union and (2) send a message to the states that were left in the new Union in case the South should prevail and the old Union die.

Was the Civil War a moral crusade? No, not by any stretch of the imagination or interpretation of the facts. Was the Civil War fought to free the slaves? Again, No!; not by any stretch of the imagination or interpretation of the facts. Was the Civil War fought over slavery? That is a very vague question and, therefore, could have been the case. Slavery was what made the Southern economy and way of life different from that of Northerners and Westerners. When looked at as an economic reality, it could be said that the war was fought over slavery. But we must be careful; there is a big difference between fighting over slavery and fighting to free the slaves. Students of history can not fail to clearly understand that distinction.

If the North had started the war, it could be argued that the war was fought to free the slaves. However, the fact of the matter is that the North (1) did not start the war, (2) was ready and willing to legitimize slavery throughout the country to keep the South from seceding and (3) was even prepared to discourage individuals from promoting abolitionist activities. Additionally, Northerners had not freed the Blacks in the North because Northerners despised Black People as much as Southerners did. No, Northerners were not willing to go to war to fight for the freedom of the slaves. The Civil War, the War Between the States, had absolutely nothing to do with freeing the Black human beings who were enslaved in practically every section of the United States of America. The War Between the States was all about economics and politics.

Slavery became a bigger factor during the war than it had ever been in the years prior to the war. Before the war, there were only two major players and two critical arenas involved in this drama. The major players were the North and the South, and the two critical arenas were the economic and the political. During the war, a third major player emerged, as did a third critical arena. The third major player was the slave, and the third critical arena was the military. These two additions took the proceedings of the Civil War out of the hands of hot-headed Northern and Southern whites. By the time the whites became aware of this huge change, the slaves had freed themselves and placed themselves in a position to determine which economic and political forces would win the war between the states and which would lose it.

IV. They Fight The War

When he was inaugurated in 1861, Abraham Lincoln became the 16th President of the United States. Abraham Lincoln would have eliminated abolitionists before he would have eliminated slavery. Because forces came into play that neither Northerners or Southerners could have predicted, he didn't have to do either.

Lincoln did not want to start a war with the South, so he waited and bided his time after the South demanded the surrender of Fort Sumter. Once the South fired on Fort Sumter, Lincoln was able to appeal to the patriotic emotions of those who remained in the Union and legitimize a military response. This patriotic response was not to last long, however, and the ability of the North to sustain an effective military campaign would be undermined as a result.

After considering all of the usual factors, it is easy to conclude that the South should have won the Civil War. Wall Street certainly thought so (it boomed every time the South reported a victory), as did most observers in the United States, France and England. One factor favored the South more than any other: it did not have to conquer the North. In order to win the war, the North had to conquer the South, but all the South had to do was hold on until the North gave up the fight. For most of the first two years, the South was doing more than holding on, it was defeating the Northern armies on a consistent basis. If the North had given up the fight, as many Northerners wanted to do, the war would have been over. However, Abraham Lincoln was not willing to give up the fight.

In addition to only having to defend its own ground, the South benefitted from the fact that the North's top military commanders and its everyday soldiers regularly handicapped the North's military response. It soon became evident that whites who supported the North were not willing to fight to the extent needed to win a war, particularly if they suspected that the war was being fought to free the slaves. Additionally, the North's early commanders were not made of the stock that the situation called for. This was the opposite of the initial fervor with which the Southerners fought and the brilliance and audacity of the South's commanders, and the consequences were clearly to the South's liking.

By the second year of the war, it seemed that the effort to preserve the Union would not succeed. President Lincoln and the Union forces needed something to happen that would turn the tide to the North's favor. Although Lincoln would not acknowledge it, what the North needed had started to gain momentum as soon as the war began. The slaves, who made up the economic backbone of the South, were also the key to the South's war effort. No one had taken this into account, and this is the factor all of the odds makers had failed to consider when they concluded that the South would win the war. What a glaring oversight that turned out to be.

With the start of the war, it became clear that the Southern slave system did not have enough white men to enforce slavery and fight the war at the same time. Feeling that the slaves were stupid and would fail to take advantage of the opportunity, the Southerners took them for granted and concentrated on the war. At that point, what the slaves decided to do was more important than any other factor in determining which side would win the war. If the slaves were to act stupid and continue to carry out their duties on the plantations, the South would win the war. But if the slaves did otherwise, the South would have no chance of maintaining the old South, even if the South still somehow managed to win the war.

The response of the slaves was immediate. Realizing that no one was present to bring down the weight of the system against them, they rebelled and began abandoning the plantations in droves. They ran to Northern armies and offered their services to the Northern military effort. This shift of Black energy from the South to the North relieved the South of its "bread and butter" and delivered the same to the North. All of a sudden, it was not the North that was staring defeat in the face, it was the South. When Lincoln put more pressure on the South by issuing the Emancipation Proclamation, the Southern way of life was doomed. Even if the South somehow managed to win the war, they would not be able to return the slaves to the plantations or keep the slaves who remained in the South from "escaping" to the North. As soon as the slaves began abandoning the plantations in large numbers, astute Southerners like Robert E. Lee and Northerners like Abraham Lincoln knew that the old South had "gone with the wind."

Contrary to what is always taught, the Emancipation Proclamation did not free the slaves. What the Emancipation proclamation did was recognize the facts that (1) the slaves were already freeing themselves and (2) their value to the Northern war effort was incalculable. By encouraging more slaves to abandon the plantations, Lincoln could deal a hard blow to the Southern war effort, and that is exactly what he did.

The North won the war because Abraham Lincoln would not quit the fight. There were several times when the fight looked hopeless, when he could have screamed "uncle" and nobody would have been critical of him for doing so. If it had been a simple matter of freedom for the slaves, Lincoln would undoubtedly have thrown in the towel before the war was two years old. But freedom for Black People was not the issue to Lincoln, preserving the Union was. Because of that, Lincoln was willing to continue the fight into eternity. After the slaves began abandoning the plantations, Lincoln realized he had three things going for him; (1) numbers (if he could convince Northern whites to enlist in the army and fight), (2) finances (to pay for the war, a Bureau of Internal Revenue taxed Americans on their incomes for the first time, brokers who hoped to sell war bonds and securities opened Wall Street up to the average person for the first time, and the federal government "went to bed" with Wall Street in order to get loans and other sources of financing. The South did not have these options to comparable degrees), and (3) time. The blockade of the South that was established as soon as the war began and augmented by what was effectively the first submarine had little or no impact on the South up to this point. But with more and more slaves leaving the plantations, it would be only a matter of time before privation would cripple the Southern spirit more than any military offensive could. Additionally, those commanders capable of leading the Northern war effort were now emerging and fighting the war as it should have been fought all along. As time and numbers took their toll, the roles were effectively reversed. By the end of the second year, it was not the South that could win by simply holding on, it was the North.

But the North did more than hold on, it took control. With its infrastructure abandoning the plantations, the South was capable of only one thing; imminent collapse. The South began a fight against time. It hoped for a huge military victory or innovation that would dishearten the North and end the war. It got a couple of impact victories, but nothing that would cause Lincoln to quit. Realizing that Lincoln would never quit, Robert E. Lee made the most brilliant military move of the entire war by surrendering to Ulysses S. Grant at the Appomattox Court House in McLean, Virginia. The Civil War had ended right outside of Washington, DC, only a few miles from where its first major battle had occurred. All things considered, the South was not that bad off. It had failed to successfully secede, but Lee had placed it in a position that enabled it to maintain its way of life.

V. Where Does White Power Go From Here?

The South was not repentant, but it realized it had taken a magnificent gamble and lost. The loss was magnificent not so much for its audacity as for its stupidity. With hindsight, they could see that their best move would have been to relent when their brothers and sisters up north had been willing to concede to all of the South's demands. But Southerners wanted to eat their cake and have it too. They didn't have the time to eat it before hostilities began, and by the time hostilities had ended, their cake was in the hands of their brothers and sisters from the North.

As they looked back, miscalculation after miscalculation haunted them. Southern secessionists were certain that Northerners would not fight, and if they fought, they would not do so for long. They never imagined that anyone would be able to raise the passions of Northerners around preserving the Union, as Lincoln was able to do. Southerners never thought that Northerners would stoop so low as to bring Black soldiers and military personnel in on a quarrel that involved white men, but the North preferred using Blacks to losing the war. Also, it never occurred to Southerners that Great Britain could do without their cotton and stay out of the war, but Great Britain did quite well with the cotton it had in reserve. And, Southern secessionists did not realize far enough in advance that they did not have a strong enough infrastructure to support a war and enforce a slave system at the same time. Trying to support two ain't easy to do, the South learned. What a costly lesson that was.

But the biggest mistake Southerners made was to believe in the mythology they had concocted about slaves and Black People in general. They literally fell victim to their own propaganda. They were stupid enough to convince themselves that the slaves really were happy, that the ones who ran away suffered from a mental illness, that Blacks were incapable of critical or intelligent thought, that Blacks had more in common with chattel than humans and that free Blacks were more prone to suffer from insanity than enslaved Blacks. Southerners had actually convinced themselves that, given the choice between slavery and freedom, Blacks would recognize that they could not handle the responsibility of freedom and choose slavery; between staying on the plantation and leaving, Blacks would choose to stay; between fighting for the South to preserve slavery and fighting for the North, Blacks would choose to fight for the South. It was this miscalculation, more than any other, that Southerners could not come to grips with, did not come to grips with.

As they looked forward, Southerners could not come to grips with the fact that, after all was said and done, it was Black People who had thwarted their move for independence. "Niggas" who had refused to stay in "their place" had tilted an argument between white men in favor of the North. How could slaves make the type of self serving decisions any human being would be expected to make, especially when they knew how much Southerners depended on them to act like they were "supposed" to act? How could they betray the Southern cause so completely, and with such total conviction? And what gave them the nerve to think that they had the right to leave "their place," interfere in a battle between "honorable" white men, try to destroy the Southern way of life, and convert the battle into a crusade for their own freedom? Southerners concluded that they would accommodate themselves to the demands made by their whites conquerors from the North, but they would not accommodate themselves to a new arrangement with Black People.

Thus it was that, on the eve of Appomattox, Robert E. Lee decided that it was time to terminate a war that had spiralled out of control and now pitted white Northerners and Blacks against white Southerners. Fundamental changes had taken place during the war that had to be reckoned with. On the one hand, even if the South were to somehow emerge victorious, Southerners would not be able to re-establish slavery to the extent it had existed prior to the war because defiant Northern whites would certainly organize under the banner of abolitionism and help slaves escape in such large numbers that the system would be ruined. So a Southern victory, in effect, meant not only the end of slavery, but perpetual conflict between Northern and Southern whites. On the other hand, to continue the fight and surrender later would only deepen the cleavage between Northern and Southern whites and render any worthwhile degree of future collaboration that much more difficult. Lee decided that it was time to begin laying the foundation for the re-emergence of the long standing and safer war Northern and Southern white people had been waging against Black People. The North could not be forced to give up the advances it had made during the course of the war, but if

Southern and Northern whites co-operated with one another, Black People could be put back into "their place."

In spite of the damage generated by the hostilities, Robert E. Lee knew that white Northerners would prefer to ally themselves with white Southerners who had recently rebelled than Black slaves who had recently helped the North win the war. He waved the white flag, let go of the white establishment that had governed the South in the past, and set the stage for the evolution of a new Southern white power reality. If it was not intended to be a stroke of genius, it certainly turned out that way. Robert E. Lee, the most revered Confederate of all, had given the South a reason to lick its wounds and charge into the future.

Chapter 24:
RECONSTRUCTING WHITE POWER
I. The Shot That Ended The War

Long before the Civil War ended, Abraham Lincoln recognized the need for a brotherly reunion between the warring sections. He therefore began formulating a policy for bringing the rebellious states back into the Union once they had been defeated. Lincoln's preference was to act as if the rebellion left no remnants of discord or bad tastes in anyone's mouth. He wanted to re-admit every Southern state to the Union with full privileges just as soon as 10% of each state's citizens had sworn allegiance to the Union and organized a new state government. Why 10%? Because the United States of America is a country that is dominated by a minority of its citizens. "Majority rule" is one of white America's most popular slogans, and it is good for propaganda purposes; but the reality is that white America has never functioned based on the will of the majority. Lincoln knew quite well that a small minority supported by the weight of the government apparatus is what rules America. What Lincoln needed in the South were a few Southern citizens who were willing to accept defeat, start over and act the way the victorious North wanted them to act. These, supported by the weight of the national government, could create a status quo that would force the South's majority to either toe the line or endure severe repercussions. Lincoln realized that, sooner or later, most would reluctantly toe the line.

Unfortunately for Lincoln, Lee's surrender did not end the war in everybody's mind. A last gasp conspiracy to save the South resulted in the simultaneous assassination of Lincoln and attempted assassination of William Seward, his Secretary of State. Seward's assailant ran into unexpected opposition and only managed to wound him. Lincoln's assailant was undeterred. As death gradually consumed the President, his plans for reconstructing the country faded from the agenda of most politicians.

The Reconstruction process would not have been the

same if Abraham Lincoln had lived, but it would not have been as different as many people tend to think. As I stated in a previous chapter, the history of the United States of America is not driven by individuals, but by a combination of forces that lie at the core of this country's raison d'etre (reason for being). These forces would have insisted on their rights even if Lincoln had lived, and they would have forced Lincoln to make concessions that he might not have wanted to make. With Lincoln's death, however, these forces did not have to confront a political opponent that was clear-minded, determined and guided by a carefully thought out plan. They had to confront much less than that. As a result, they were able to impact on and take control of the Reconstruction process more easily than they would have if Lincoln had not been assassinated.

Additionally, in spite of his educated qualities, Abraham Lincoln was a white man, first and foremost. His mission was to preserve the Union that had been established by his revered white forefathers, and he was determined to do that at whatever cost. In order to preserve the Union he had refused to stop fighting a war that seemed impossible to win, and having won the war, would not have allowed anything less than an American pillar to keep the sections from reuniting in a brotherly way. Although many might not have realized it at the time, all of the major historical incompatibilities between the North and South had been eliminated by the war. The incompatibility that ignited the war, that of labor, had been resolved to the favor of Northern capitalism; unpaid labor would no longer exist. The war also eliminated the schisms caused by arguments over the tariff, congressional representation, whether slavery was territorial or national and resumption of the Atlantic slave trade. In fact, if white people had had their way, the war would have ended all hostility between Northern and Southern whites. But white people lost control of the war and, during that lapse, the slaves managed to free themselves. Thus, the war, in the process of eliminating all of the old incompatibility issues, generated an entirely new issue that was capable of keeping Northern and Southern whites at each other's throats. That issue revolved around what role the former slaves, and Black People in general, were to play in the new Union. Lincoln preferred to colonize Black People but discovered that was an impossibility. As a result, he might have orated in the interest of Black People, but if push had come to shove, and it certainly would have, Lincoln, as Robert E. Lee well knew, would have subjugated the concerns of Black People and given priority to those of Southern whites.

That, unfortunately, is understandable. Abraham Lincoln was a man who, in his mid- fifties, had never had any appreciable personal or social contact with any Black individuals. His opposition to slavery was purely philosophical, as would have been whatever post-war support he might have mustered for Black People. Philosophy, alas, is the type of pristine stuff that often falters when faced with cruel political realities, and white America is replete with cruel realities. Lincoln's stance would not have been supported by anything as substantial or mythologically forceful as the bigoted and racist environment he lived in from the day he was born until the day he died. His objective logic would not have been able to withstand the bigotry and racism that had permeated the land and white people since the arrival of Cristobal Colon. His philosophical resistance might have tried to take a stand, but would have tottered and then collapsed under the weight and energy of white America's cruel realities. There is no guarantee that Lincoln would have tried to be righteous with Black People, but if he had, he would have discovered that Robert E. Lee knew him better than he knew himself. From the day Robert E. Lee surrendered, Reconstruction was a done deal. The only thing to be determined was how Reconstruction would evolve into what it was preordained to be.

II. Reconstruction: A False Start

When Lee waved the flag of surrender, the North was ecstatic. The thrill of victory engulfed not only astute politicians but disappointed businessmen as well. And the North remained ecstatic, but as the days passed into weeks, Northerners began to come to grips with some uneasy political and economic implications of that victory. It had forced the South back into the Union, but what, exactly, did that mean? What did it mean politically, economically and socially?

The minds of Northern politicians flashed back to all of the age-old incompatibilities that caused friction between the Northern and Southern states. Would there be a resumption of the perennial political tug of war to determine which section would control the national government? Would there be a resumption of the economic battle between Northern capitalism and Southern capitalism? How would whites from the North and South relate to each other after trying to maim and kill each other for so long a time? Would the South be able to set aside the deaths and bitterness and adjust to Northern priorities? And what about Black People? Without them, the North would not have won the war! What was to be their reward or compensation, if any, and where did they now stand in white America's overall scheme of things?

Northern politicians were adamant about one thing: the North had won the war, and there was to be no doubt that the national government would favor the interests of the loyal Union states. Under the re-united government, it would be the North dictating the terms and the South conforming to those dictates-- that was beyond discussion! But was it? Whether the North would be able to dictate terms or not would be determined by the conditions under which the South returned to the Union. If the South returned with the same amount of status that it possessed before seceding, that would be unnerving but acceptable because the balance of power was clearly in the hands of free states now, by a comfortable majority. But the South could not return under the same conditions that existed when it left because the Blacks in the South were free people now. That meant that the population basis of representation in the South was noticeably greater. Since the 3/5 clause no longer applied to Blacks, the Black population in the South, congressionally speaking, had instantly increased by 40%! As a result, more Southerners would be seated in Congress now than before the South seceded from the Union! Was it wise to allow the states that had seceded from the Union to rejoin the Union with more political clout than they had ever had before? And, even more importantly, could Southern planters who had lost the war use these additional congressional seats to prompt a coalition with Westerners and gain control of the national government-- the national government that had just defeated them in war? This thought unnerved Northerners practically to no end. As impossible as it seemed, it was conceivable that the North, which had won the war, could lose control of the government to the very rebels they had just defeated on the battlefield. Northern politicians were determined that that would not be allowed to happen.

The dictates of Northern capitalism made one thing certain: a system of slave labor would not be tolerated. Henceforth, capitalists would rid themselves of any responsibility for the well being of laborers, expand their production and marketing zones of influence and bathe in the additional profits this new arrangement would generate. Thus, it is noteworthy that the first major piece of legislation proposed after the close of the war was the 13th Amendment to the constitution. Contrary to what has been popularly taught, the 13th Amendment did not free the slaves (the slaves had already freed themselves). What the 13th Amendment did was recognize what was an accomplished fact and place the country's stamp of recognition on that accomplishment.

Legal recognition of that accomplishment was of momentous importance to Northern capitalism. That helps explain why the 13th Amendment was an essentially economic measure; the first of many that would clarify what was only hinted at in the original constitution; that Northern capitalism was in fact the supreme law of the land. The newly free Black People would increase the congressional power of the South whether an amendment recognizing their freedom were passed or not, so there was no risk involved in recognizing their freedom as a matter of law. Recognizing their freedom did not infer anything else, and certainly was not meant to be an omen of imminent political or social elevation for the former slaves. The 13th Amendment carried one essential message, and one message only: Northern capitalism had defeated Southern capitalism, and a free labor market throughout the country was the reward the North received for acquiring that victory.

The 13th Amendment was not a Reconstruction measure, nor was it a moral or political event by any stretch of the imagination. We have already discussed the lack of morals that pervaded this country enough to not go further into that, but it must be made clear that politics played only a minor role in its passage. If politics had been at the core of the 13th Amendment, it would have been followed quickly by a second such amendment or political initiative; one that recognized the political rights and options of the Black People who had recently freed themselves. No such political initiative or amendment was forthcoming. That is because white America had no intention of awarding Black People any domestic political status or of acknowledging the political rights the Blacks now possessed as a free and independent people. The 13th Amendment was passed because it was to white America's economic advantage to pass it. White Northerners, just as Robert E. Lee had intuitively known, were not concerned about what was to evolve between Northern whites and Black People. The only concern of Northern whites revolved around the new, emerging relationship between themselves and Southern whites.

Consistent with the priorities of Northern capitalism was a second piece of legislation, that which created the

Freedmen's Bureau. The Freedmen's Bureau sought to provide Black People with a minimal education and force the former slaves to do plantation work on a wage labor basis. A labor force that is literate is an advantage to a capitalist system of the type championed by Northern businessmen because it tends to increase the level of efficiency of the laborers. Additionally, Northern businessmen knew that a ready labor supply would be a boost to the Southern economy and a reminder to Southern planters that white Northerners continued to view them as brothers and wanted to see them prosper under the new economic arrangement.

Andrew Johnson, Lincoln's successor as president, tried to implement Lincoln's plan and pacify Northern capitalism as best he could. Since Congress was not in session when the war ended, Johnson proceeded to re-admit the Southern states without Congress' input. As a result, by the time Congress was to meet, several of the Southern states had already complied with the requirements for re-admission to the Union; they had satisfied the 10% requirement, established new governments that expressed their loyalty to the Union and elected new congressional representatives. But, when Congress convened in December of 1865, it refused to allow any of those members to take their seats, opened an investigation into political and social conditions in the Southern states, passed a Civil Rights bill over the veto of President Johnson and made it crystal clear that the South had to make some fundamental changes and concessions before it was allowed to become a fully privileged member of the Union again.

III. Congress Takes Control

As was recently stated, Northern politicians were adamant about one thing: the North had won the war, and there was to be no doubt that the national government would favor the interests of the loyal Union states. Under the re-united government, it would be the North dictating the terms and the South conforming to those dictates-- that was beyond discussion. Since it was certain that the South would return to the Union with more power than it had had when it seceded, Northern politicians had to diagram a Reconstruction policy that would ensure Southern compliance with Northern priorities. How to do that???- that was the question the victorious North had to find the answer to!

There was also a lesser question that some Northern politicians felt obligated to address. What was to be Black People's reward or compensation, if any, for the role they had played in preserving the Union? The 13th Amendment had addressed the economic needs of Northern capitalism by making freedom for the slaves a legal reality, but there was no political substance to that measure. Nor was there any political substance to the Freedmen's Bureau. The fact of the matter was that white people, both Northern and Southern, never seriously thought of political rights and Black People in the same breath. Black People's sole reason for existing was to serve the interests of white people. That was the way it had been and, in the minds of almost every white person, that was the way it would always be.

Northern politicians, with the exception of a handful of individuals like Charles Sumner and Thaddeus Stevens, had no intention of introducing a political element to the reality of Black People in the United States. American politicians knew that, as free people, no existing government could legally tell Black People what to do. They knew that, as a free people, Black People had the right to take control of their own political destiny. It had been nearly four years since Blacks had begun freeing themselves, and more than a year since the 13th Amendment had recognized that accomplishment. Black People had been a free and independent people living in the United States for all that time! It was beyond argument: politically speaking, no one had the right to tell them what they could or could not do.

In spite of that, Northern politicians were not willing

to tell the former slaves what political options were available to them. They knew that, as a free people, Black People had four political options: Black People could (1) seek United States citizenship, (2) return to Africa at the expense of the United States, (3) emigrate to another country at the expense of the United States or (4) set up an independent, self-governing nation of their own on land that was presently a part of the United States of America. Northern politicians were totally against the first and fourth options, and unwilling to pay for the other two options. They therefore decided to not inform Black People of their options, and, in so doing, left Black People in the political limbo they had been in since they had begun freeing themselves.

But Northern politicians were not to leave Black People in limbo for long. Northern politicians wanted political supremacy over the South more than anything else. However, the new governments that had been established under Lincoln and Johnson's plan were composed of the same old plantation types that had led the rebellion, and they immediately began to re-establish the old South as best they could. In spite of Black People's firm opposition, Southern politicians passed Black codes that effectively re-enslaved Black People, and failed to support the 14th Amendment, a Northern measure that redefined citizenship in a way that included Black People. These acts convinced Northern politicians that they had to play hardball in order to force Southerners to comply with Northern priorities. Northerners had never given any serious thought to giving Black People the power to vote, but Southern stubbornness was forcing their hand. They eventually faced up to the fact that if Black People could vote, they could help Northern politicians force the South to toe the line. Having faced up to that fact, they set the wheels in motion and prepared to use Black People in whatever capacity and to whatever extent necessary.

Once again, Black People would be the pivotal factor in a tug of war between Northern and Southern whites. Once again, Northern whites would benefit immensely,

Southern whites would react in barbaric ways toward Black People, and Black People would remain in political limbo and suffer the consequences.

IV. The Reconstruction Amendments

Since the 3/5 clause no longer applied to Blacks, the Black population in the South, congressionally speaking, had increased by 40%! Unless something were done to upset the implications of that formula, more Southern planters would be seated in Congress after the war than before the South seceded from the Union! Northern politicians devised a three step process that could keep this from happening. The first step was to deny office holding privileges to white men in the South who had rebelled against the Union. The second was to give voting privileges to the Blacks who had freed themselves during the war (Blacks would vote the way Northern congressmen wanted them to vote). And the third? To militarily occupy the South until steps one and two had convinced Southerners that they had to comply with Northern policies before they could get back at the former slaves. This three step process lies at the core of the Reconstruction policy of Northern congressmen, and it manifested itself in the proposal and ratification of the 14th and 15th Amendments to the United States constitution.

The 14th Amendment used language that recognized Black People as citizens of the United States, threatened the South with a reduction of congressional representation if eligible persons were not allowed to vote and denied office holding privileges to those who had rebelled against the Union. As a citizenship measure for Black People, it was illegal because, as a free people, Black People could not be made citizens of the United States without their prior consent and without having been made aware of all of the political options that were open to them. White politicians treated that legality as if it were merely a technicality. Like white people before them,

Northern politicians were quite capable of ignoring the law when it was to their advantage to do so.

In order to make the 14th Amendment serve its politically motivated purpose, the 15th Amendment was proposed within months after the 14th was ratified. The 15th Amendment gave Black People the right to vote. Thus, in two short strokes, Congress turned the Black presence in the South from a potential advantage for Southern planters to a powerful weapon wielded by Northern politicians. In every Southern state, the majority of the voting Republicans became Black men who attached their destiny to that of white Northerners, played the political role they were expected to play and worked to eliminate racism. Having the weight of the national government behind them, Black People played a role in the South that they had never been permitted to play before-- not even in the rest of the country. They voted responsibly, ran for and were elected to state and national offices, and produced some of the most progressive legislation in all of the United States. They also occupied many positions of responsibility and performed just as efficiently as white Americans had performed. These were the "mystic years" for Black People in the United States, so accurately labelled and described by W. E. B. DuBois. Finally, they had the opportunity to prove to white people that they were not human chattel, but intelligent human beings. Thenceforward, in the minds of Black People, white people would have no reason to argue that Black People were inferior to whites and incapable of managing their or anyone else's human affairs.

What the Black spokespersons of the day failed to do was make the distinction between having the weight of the government behind them and possessing power. In spite of the new roles they were allowed to play, the bottom line for Blacks remained the same: they were powerless within the white political scheme and still in political limbo. Additionally, they must have been so overwhelmed by the thought of "freedom" that it seemed to not occur to them that white people were not interested in having anything proved or disproved about Black People. Neither the whites in the North or those in the South were interested in having Black People's merits proved or disproved. White Northerners were simply using Black People to force white Southerners to toe the line according to Northern dictates. The Northern message to Southern whites was straight and clear: if you don't want Black People to continue playing a dominant role in the political and social life of the South, you had better comply with Northern dictates. And the South's response was predictable. Each day, the hatred white Southerners felt for Black People increased and their desire to put Black People back in "their place" intensified. Reconstruction, then, was a social and political tug of war that involved three parties; powerful white Northerners, powerful white Southerners and the powerless Blacks that were used as bait.

V. Blood Is Always Thicker

It was not a question of if, but when. The South had quickly began to see the benefits of a labor system that was paid (in theory if not in fact), so the interests of the proponents of Northern capitalism were getting what they wanted out of the war. Southern resistance to Reconstruction, therefore, did not have an economic element. It was strictly of a political nature, and it centered around one financial and one social objective. The financial objective was to keep land in the hands of Southern planters. The social objective was to put the niggas back in "their place."

Southern whites realized that Black People did not have the power to finance or carry out a Reconstruction policy. They knew that Black People were pawns in the hands of powerful Northerners who used them like a tool while simultaneously dangling them like bait in order to stimulate the racist juices of Southern whites. It wouldn't have been that difficult to seek revenge against their brothers up north, but they didn't feel that vengeful toward Northerners and they knew it wouldn't serve a useful purpose anyway. Why go underground, form an independent provisional government or establish anti-North guerilla cadres when they could get more satisfactory revenge at less risk by terrorizing the North's tool-- Black People? They knew they could terrorize Black People and get away with it because they knew that Reconstruction was really about the new nature of the relationship between whites in the North and whites in the South. They knew their Northern brothers had no substantial interest in the well-being of Black People, would not go out of their way to support or defend them for long and were hoping Southerners would end the whole regrettable affair by agreeing to toe the Northern line. They would toe the Northern line and make peace with their brothers eventually, but right now they would concern themselves with taking revenge out on the Northerner's tool and teaching them to stay out of white people's business.

Black People were killed, warned to not vote, and perpetually intimidated by white terrorists who belonged to organizations like the Ku Klux Klan, Knights of the White Camellia and the like. The 15th Amendment, for all intents and purposes, was rendered null and void, and the fact that they were powerless hit Black People hard and furiously. The fact that Northern whites were not intent on protecting them became clearer and clearer as the Southern attack progressed, yet the Blacks could not protect themselves because they were a despised people in political limbo. They hoped the uncaring North would protect them, yet knew the North would sympathize with white Southerners and characterize Blacks as vigilantes if Black People effectively organized and defended themselves against white people. Each day, the Southern whites got more and more aggressive and Northern whites got more and more tired of the situation. The Civil War had served its purpose as far as white Northerners were concerned. It was time to let bygones be bygones. White America had always waged a war against Black People, so what was the big deal now? It was time for white power to move on.

And white power did move on. By 1872, Reconstruction had been mortally wounded. By 1875, all of the Black militias that had played such a prominent role in the early stages of Reconstruction had been ordered to disband by the national government. This eliminated the last line of lawful self-defense for Black People. Then, in 1877, all voting and office holding privileges were returned to members of the old Southern officer class. By 1876, when Rutherford B. Hayes was running for President, all but two of the South's state governments were back in the hands of the planter class that had seceded from the Union. When Hayes agreed to remove all remaining federal troops from the South if he were made President, Reconstruction was buried and order had been restored. White power America was reunited at last; economically, politically and socially. It was time to let internal wounds heal, explore other boundaries and see what of value was in the possession of the rest of the world.

Section Four: Summary

The United States was steeped in fundamental contradictions at its birth. However, when the United States illegally overthrew the Articles of Confederation and supplanted it with a new constitution that professed free enterprise and liberty for all, it augured a nation that would be increasingly enamored of deceit and guided by hypocrisy.

The coup d'etat carried out by the makers of the U. S. constitution created a union that was "more perfect" for them. If either of the founding fathers had actually been committed to doing what was good for the people of this country, the coup d'etat of 1776, otherwise known as the American Revolution, might have matured into a genuinely revolutionary experiment in government by the people. But America's main men were too weak individually, too motivated by personal considerations and too based in a narrow view of humanity. Unfortunately, the country they became symbolic of retained all of their inadequacies.

The white Englishmen who established the new nation could not get along with each other. Rather than rally around a national picture, they remained strapped inside local and regional snapshots that rendered them incapable of magnifying their likenesses, acting in the interest of the whole and resolving their differences in a civilized manner. Because they were so incapable, the Civil War seemed inevitable, and the Civil War was fought.

The South, the home of slavery, took the step that led to the Civil War. But even as the events leading up to the Civil War seemed to revolve around slavery, slavery was not the issue. Slavery was the crutch the issue walked on, and it carried the weight so completely, so thoroughly, that it and the issue became indistinguishable in the eyes of many. In fact, the South fought the war in order to free the South and Southern capitalism, while the North fought the war in order to give Northern capitalism the freedom to dominate the entire country. During the process, the slaves freed themselves and made it possible for the North to prevail.

After the war, the whites in the North and South came to an agreement and the Blacks were put back in "their place." Northern capitalism had triumphed on the economic front, political capitalism had emerged as the new law of the land, and white elites focussed their attention on conquering the rest of the world.

Section Four: Review Questions

(1) What contradictions was the United States steeped in, even before its birth as an independent nation?

(2) Did these contradictions entrench themselves and become an essential part of white Americanism?

(3) Why is it asserted that a constitutional coup d'etat took place in the United States in 1776?

(4) Do the constitutional activities in Philadelphia in 1776 prove that revolution is not a matter of gunfire but

of who controls each individual's personal power?

(5) Who were the early pillars of hypocrisy in the United States?

(6) In Chapter 20, reference is made to "the invisible pilot." What is your understanding of that reference?

(7) Do you agree that the United States was only capable of being a "greedy, arrogant, militaristic country that rotated around business considerations?"

(8) What were some of long standing priorities and incompatibilities that had evolved since the settling of the early colonies that George Washington's administration had to deal with?

(9) What is meant when it is stated that "back and forth jockeying over non-fundamental issues typified politics in the United States for several decades, and continues today?"

(10) What is the importance of the following observation: "America's paradigm, its central motivating forces, preceded Washington's presidency, absorbed it and outlived it. It did the same thing for all of America's presidencies."

(11) Was Napoleon Bonaparte's role in the expansion of the United States legitimate?

(12) What role did the Blacks of San Domingo play in the expansion of the United States?

(13) Who were the Washitaw, and what did the Washitaw possess that the United States wanted at all costs?

(14) Why did Abraham Lincoln refer to Washitaw land as "the Egypt of the West?"

(15) In what regard was Andrew Jackson typical of white individuals in the United States?

(16) Who were America's actual modern natives?

(17) What did the United States government do to expand westward at the expense of Mexico?

(18) What role did unpaid and underpaid labor play in the prospering of white America?

(19) What role did unpaid and underpaid labor play in the advent of sectional unrest and the War Between the

States?

(20) According to "the law," was the exploitation and abuse of Native American and African labor legal? What are the implications of that?

(21) What is secession, and what role has that term played in the history of white America?

(22) Did Andrew Jackson think "the Negro, or slavery question" would be the cause of a war between the states?

(23) Give your impression of the systematic attacks waged by white America against African and Native American occupants of America.

(24) Is it correct to state that white America's reaction to Black People was psychopathic?

(25) Prior to the Civil War, what did Blacks do to convince whites that they were not content with their status as slaves?

(26) Did the frequency of slave rebellions generate a high degree of psychological instability among white Southerners?

(27) Why was the policy of neighboring countries in regard to slavery a bigger threat to slavery than even the slave rebellions?

(28) After all was said and done, where did the fate of slavery lay?

(29) Which side started the War Between the States? Does that disprove the assertion that the war was fought in order to free the slaves?

(30) What was the real reason the War Between the States was fought?

(31) When Abraham Lincoln was elected President, did he intend to free the slaves?

(32) Who freed the slaves?

(33) What advantages did the South have going into the Civil War?

(34) What advantages did the North have going into the Civil War?

(35) Why was the North able to win the war?

(36) Did the Emancipation Proclamation free the

slaves in the North?

(37) Since Abraham Lincoln was not the President of the Confederate States of America, what authority did the Emancipation Proclamation have in the South?

(38) What was Abraham Lincoln's sole purpose for fighting the Civil War?

(39) Do you think Robert E. Lee's surrender was a stroke of genius?

(40) Who were the three major players in the Reconstruction process?

(41) Did all of the major players in the Reconstruction process have power?

(42) Why is the term "bait" used to refer to Black People's role in the Reconstruction process?

(43) Blacks had proved to be the difference maker in the Civil War and the Reconstruction process. What was the response of white Northerners and white Southerners to this?

(44) As a matter of policy, did white Southerners seek revenge on white Northerners or Black People during the Reconstruction years?

(45) What did Northern capitalism want the Reconstruction process to produce?

(46) What did Northern politicians want the Reconstruction process to produce?

(47) Political capitalism became the law of the land. What is meant by that statement?

(48) What did the 13th Amendment do and what is its importance in terms of Black People being a free people?

(49) Were Northern politicians willing to tell the former slaves what political options were available to them as a free people?

(50) Black People were in political limbo during the Reconstruction period. How did that contribute to their inability to defend themselves against attacks by Southern whites?

(51) Why did northern politicians decide to make Black People citizens of the United States and give them the

right to vote?

(52) What is the difference between having the weight of the government behind you and possessing power? How was that important to Black People during the Reconstruction period, and what does it imply about Black People in the United States in the 21st century?

(53) What is the importance of "blood always being thicker" to race relations and power in the United States of America?

CONCLUSION

I. Of Business, By Business, and For Business

As W. E. B. DuBois stated so accurately, Northern capitalism conquered the South during the Civil War and, from there, went on to conquer the world. But before Northern capitalism conquered the South, Northern capitalism conquered the new government of the United States by executing a constitutional coup d'etat to supplant the Articles of Confederation. And before Northern capitalism conquered the new government of the United States, it made use of the Revolutionary War to break white America away from the reins of a European power that was too steeped in traditional economic values and practices to let capitalism run free. Capitalism was conceived in Europe and spent much of its infancy there, but it was the bosom of white America that zealously nourished capitalism and handled it with kid gloves. White Americans are the people who were primed to deprioritize humanity so that capitalism might be all that it could be, so it should not be surprising that the history of white America is the story of the diminishing of human concerns and values and the spiralling growth of a money driven complex.

With each conquest; that of the British in the 1770s, the Articles of Confederation in 1787, and the South in the 1860s, capitalism revealed more and more of itself. It was a self-absorbed, narcissistic, all-consuming entity; so unscrupulous, so disdainful of humanity, so intent on recreating everything in its own unbalanced image and eliminating everything that it could not recreate. But more than compensating for those odious drawbacks in the minds of white Americans was capitalism's intoxicating selfishness, its dedication to ego-gratification, its bounty of rewards for those who successfully prostituted themselves before it, the misleading promise of abundance for every person who applied its principles efficiently, and its self-serving and guilt absolving rationalizations. People enamored themselves of capitalism, even as it trivialized all of the virtues that were once so dear to them.

While white America nursed capitalism and protected it from its detractors, capitalism propelled white America's growth, multiplied white America's riches and, characteristically, made white America in its own image. White America became the epitome, the living embodiment, of an all-consuming economic ideology. Its self-absorption, narcissism and lack of scruples drove white America to pursue what it wanted by whatever means imaginable; hook or crook, intrigue or misdeed, murder or unjustified military action. Its de-prioritizing of people and humane considerations is so blatant that it causes humanitarians to shudder, and its detachment from qualities such as justice and fair play is as total as it can be at any given time. But white Americans are in love with their nation; its intoxicating selfishness, its dedication to self-gratification, the bounty of rewards it offers to those who successfully prostitute themselves before it; its self-serving propaganda and guilt absolving rationalizations were exactly what white Americans were looking for. And as they looked outward, toward the rest of the world after Reconstruction, spreading democracy was one of the least of white American's objectives. What they wanted was to spread and profit from capitalism; economic capitalism, political capitalism and social capitalism.

II. Economic Capitalism, Political Capitalism And Social Capitalism

Business, business, business; that's all capitalism cares about. It started out innocently enough, simply looking to get its foot in the financial door so it could increase an entrepreneur's returns. But the more returns it generated, the more returns it wanted to generate. And to be all that it could be, it had to remake its competitors in its own image or disparage them. It discovered that some competitors were essentially economic; non-capitalist systems (free enterprise, socialism, "communism," e.g.) and non-capitalist business structures. But economic competitors were not the only competitors. Some were essentially political (long entrenched systems of government, diplomacy and international civility) and others were essentially social (humane standards of conduct and principles based on the belief in notions like human caring, respect, justice and honesty). To reach full maturity and be all that it could be, capitalism would have to supplant all of these options and rid them of any absolute significance in the minds of people. That was capitalism's goal, it implied capitalism's modus operandi and it became the model of models for the United States as it formulated domestic and foreign policies after the end of Reconstruction .

As the United States looked outward, its economy, politics and social make-up revolved around business. White America's treatment of Native Americans and Africans had demonstrated its capacity to elevate commerce and denigrate human beings, so it was par for the course when corporations became persons and people became markets, consumers, employees, voters and other such statistical categories. The shift was ever more evident as the activities of business began to take on the assumption of legality whereas the rights of the people would have to be determined by legal proceedings. Progress and growth began losing its human context; profits, losses, gross national products and other strictly commercial assessments took their place. The aspirations of large businesses became the "national interest," Pennsylvania Avenue took its cue from Wall Street and the nation's capital played second fiddle to New York City. Education and health, charity and impartiality, worship and benevolence; all were reduced to two constants---dollars and cents. Domestic and foreign policy were not driven by the public welfare, but highly funded, bottom line driven special interest groups. As such, political elections could not be won by the best qualified individual, but the best bankrolled one, and standard operating diplomatic procedure consisted of paying other countries to abandon their traditions, principles and values. Even individuals became less a member of the human family and increasingly a financial asset or liability whose worth was determined by how s/he applied standard capitalist principles not only on the job, but to his or her personal, family and community relationships as well.

Thus, in barely more than 100 years, white America had been converted from a colony that was steered down the capitalist path to a country full of individuals who were totally absorbed by capitalistic principles. This is the white America that looked toward the world after 1877. Her conduct from that time to the present has been arrogant, predictable, capitalistically single-minded and, all too often, deplorable.

III. And The Future?

The colonies that were to become the United States of America started off as little businesses; as individual proprietorships, partnerships and corporations. They evolved into pillars of capitalism, an economic system that does not hinge on democratic principles and is not concerned about creating environments that promote equality and human justice. So, what white Americans should do, what ALL Americans must do, is ask themselves if it is indeed best for capitalism to lead the way when a social structure is supposed to be of the people, by the people and for the people. Certainly, business principles that focus on a bottom line of profits and losses are the worst principles to serve as the basis for establishing a socially responsible, human-centric status quo.

White America's attachment to capitalism and the white mythology, and its unwarranted sense of superiority have not allowed white Americans to honestly and objectively revisit those areas they most need to revisit. Until white Americans become capable of critically analyzing their values and what their nation has become, there is little, if anything, white America is likely to do that can help make the world a better place for human beings.

INDEX

Abolition 34
Adams, John 37, 121
Adams, Sam 37
Africa 41, 42, 118, 135, 188
African slave trade 99, 100, 139, 144, 156
Allan, Ethan 69, 72
Alexander the Great 42
Allegheny Mountains 54
Ambivalence 80
Amendments 82, 91, 92, 94
America 87
American colonialism 125
American identity 59
Americanism 106
American revolution 94, 107
Americans 13, 67, 68
Ammunition 64
Annapolis 94
Anti-Federalists 110
Anti-slavery 149
Appomattox Court House 163
Arabic 147
Arawaks 10
Arguments 57
Arnold, Benedict 67, 69
Arrogance 20
Article 1 99
Article 4 99
Article 5 99

Article 11 93
Article 13 91
Article 14 93
Article 16 93
Articles of Confederation 73-82, 83, 86-88, 91, 96, 101, 107, 180
Austin, Stephen F. 134
Bait 178
Balance of power 155, 170
Belief system 25
Bill of rights 97, 112
Black 46
Black codes 175
Black mythology 164
Black nationahood 175
Black People 143, 174
Black soldiers 164
Black states 149
Bleeding Kansas 156
Boston Massacre 37
Boston Tea Party 56
Boundaries 22, 25
Bows and arrows 131
British East India Company 37
Brown, John 156
Brown University 143
Buffalo 131
Business 27, 59, 82, 186
Businessmen 15,

75, 87, 93, 94
Business principles 189
Capitalism 30, 31, 32, 87, 119, 186, 187, 188, 189
Catholic Church 42
Central motivating forces 124
Cherokees 132
Chinese 137
Christianity 120
Church 13, 14, 20, 27
Church, Dr. Benjamin 63
Citizenship 175, 176
Civil Rights 173
Civil War 138, 140, 141, 154, 158, 181
Colonial Army 64
Colonies 14, 30
Colonizing 24, 169
Columbus , Christopher 10
Commodity 89
Communism 187
Concord 68, 72
Confederate States of America 157
Congress 73, 76, 95, 173
Constitution 91, 95, 97, 105
Consumers 87
Continental Congress 37, 56, 63, 69, 70, 71, 72, 73
Contradictions 106
Cotton 30, 86
Coup d'etat 62, 96, 101, 107, 109, 117, 180

Cristobal Colon 10, 12, 19, 42, 43, 130

Cristoforo Colombo 10

Crittenden compromise 157

Cumberland County 132

Currency Act 37, 55

Dark Ages 30

David 63, 67

Davis, Jefferson 157

Decimation 130, 131

Declaration of Rights 71

De-construct 20

Dehumanizing humanity 115

De-legitimize 20

Democratic principles 189

Democratic-Republicans 110

Differences 57

Disconnecting 16, 17

Discontentment 53, 81

Disinterested attachment 80

Distrust 76, 98

Dominican Republic 10

Dred Scott 140, 156

DuBois, W. E. B. 177, 186

Dutch 32, 50

Duty Act 56

Economic capitalism 187

Economics 124

Economic genocide 135

Education 17, 19, 20, 132

Efficiency of operations 45, 51

Electoral college 100

Elimination 26

Elites 20, 31, 62, 78, 80, 88, 93

Emancipation Proclamation 161, 162

Emigrate 175

Energy 60, 65, 148

Englishmen 14

England 13, 86, 160

Enslavement 130

Equality 120

Equal Rights Amendment 92

Europe's masses 16, 18

Everyday people 36, 61, 62, 78, 79, 80, 83

Extermination 42, 43, 130, 131, 133

External security 33

Fame 132

Farmers 30

Fear 23

Federalists 110

15th Amendment 176, 177, 179

Filipino 137

Financial thefts 135

Foreign Affairs Department 74

14th Amendment 176

Fort Sumter 158, 160

Fort Ticonderoga 69, 72

Fortuitous developments 19, 28

Fortune 133

Founding fathers 11, 12, 14, 22, 38

France 67, 117, 118, 160

Freedmen's Bureau 173

Free enterprise 86, 87

Free market 87

Free territory 152

Free the slaves 159, 161, 168

French and Indian War 64

Fugitive Slave Act 156, 157

Fugitive slave clause 100

Future 189

Gamblers 22, 38

Genocide 132

Georgia 139

God 23

Goliath 63, 67

Governments 61

Granada 123

Grant, Ulysses S 163

Great Britain 36, 50, 53, 63, 70, 71, 88, 117, 118, 164

Great Seal 74

Greed 20

Green Mountain Boys 72

Guadeloupe Hidalgo 134
Haiti 10, 118, 127
Half-way patriots 37
Hamilton, Alexander 94, 110, 111
Hancock, John 63
Hanson, John 74
Harper's Ferry 156
Hawaii 123
Hayes, Rutherford B 180
Herodotus 42
Heros 63
Hispaniola 10
Historians 13, 33, 38, 125, 137, 154
Holland 51
House of Burgesses 56
Hypocrisy 20, 106
Ideological 18
Ideological infra-structure 116
Immigrants 136
Incompatibilities 56
Independence 57
Independent gov-ernment 151
Independent minds 18
Indian 73, 83, 126, 129
Indigo 30, 48
Industrial revolution 85, 90, 91, 144
Information 19
Injun 26
Insurrections 100
Internal Revenue 162
Internal security 33

Interstate com-merce 96, 100
Intolerable Acts 37, 56
Invisible Pilot 116, 122, 168
Jackson , Andrew 132, 140, 155
Jamestown 24, 26, 27, 29, 135
Jefferson, Thomas 110, 111, 114, 127, 128
Jeffersonians 110
John Smith 28
Johnson, Andrew 173
Kansas 139, 155
Kennedys 52
King George 80
King John 25, 31
Kingship 79
Knights of the White Camellia 179
Ku Klux Klan 179
Labor 32, 45, 57, 58, 100, 135
Laborers 15, 136
Labor systems 30, 38, 98, 119
Labor unions 137
Lee, Robert E. 162, 165, 166
Legality 136
Lexington 68
Lincoln, Abraham 74, 129, 157, 159, 162, 167-169
Liquor 30, 49
Localization 75
Louisiana Territory 126, 127, 128, 129
L'Ouverture, Toussaint 127

Madison, James 94, 110, 112
Magna Carta 25, 31
Majority rule 167
Major players 159
Malcontents 15
Manifest destiny 120, 134
Manipulate the system 81
Marketing experts 47
Maroon 149, 150
Maryland 70
Massachusetts 71
Massachusetts Provincial Congress 37
Mass migration 149
Mayflower Compact 24
Merchants 25
Mexico 118, 134
Michael Milken 52
Misinformation 17, 19
Mississippi River 139
Missouri 139
Missouri Compro-mise 155
Modus operandi 122
Molasses 30, 49, 55
Money 36, 37, 38, 53
Money crop 28, 45, 48, 101
Money Products 48, 101
Money Services 48, 49, 101
Monuments 134

Morality 34, 38, 50, 123, 124, 141, 158
More perfect union 109
Mother country 53
Mutual distastes 57
Mystic years 177
NapoleonBonaparte 126-128
National bank 111
Native Americans 10, 23, 26, 39, 43, 83, 118, 119, 125, 126, 130, 131, 135, 136, 188
Nebraska 155
Netherlands 88
New Amsterdam 49, 50, 89
New Jersey 30
New York 30, 49, 88
Niggas 165
Norfolk 72
North 154, 155
North Carolina 70
Northern capitalism 99, 110, 121, 140, 142, 171, 181, 186
Northwest 124
Northwest Ordinance 108, 109, 125
Northwest Territory 109, 125
Nullification 139, 140
Office Holders 117
Oriental 137
Original People 41
Other persons 99
Overpopulation 27
Paid labor 47

Parliament 56, 70
Passive disconnectedness 80
Patriotism 61
Peers 16, 18, 20, 22
Peons 16, 18, 20, 22
Pennsylvania 30
Perpetual union 75
Perseverance 23
Perspectives 22
Philadelphia 71, 94
Philip Morris 52
Philippines 123
Philosophy 169
Pillars 20
Pioneers 22
Planters 30
Plymouth Rock 133, 135
Pocahontas 27, 28
Policies 117
Political capitalism 12, 20, 52, 187
Political disadvantage 19
Political limbo 176
Political options 175
Political parties 110, 119, 120
Polk, James Polk 134
Pontiac 36, 54
Pontiac's War 54, 55
Power 133
Powhatan 27
Pre-revolutionary 30
Pretext 140
Proclamation of 1763 36

Profits 58
Propaganda 61, 132, 164
Proprietorships 24
Pro-Slavery 99
Prosser, Gabriel 147
Provisional Government 71
Psychological instability 151
Puerto Rico 123
Punishment 142
Puritans 57
Quakers 63
Quartering Act 37, 55
Racial propaganda 41
Ratification 92, 94, 100, 112
Rebellers 148
Reconstruction 167, 169, 170, 176, 178
Red Americans 41
Religion 50, 124
Religious conversion 27
Religious doctrines 27
Republic of New Afrika 71
Revolutionary War 36, 62, 66
Rice 30, 48
RJ Reynolds 52
Rotisserie style 145
Rum 30
Runaway slaves 157
Samoset 27

San Domingo 118, 126, 127
Saratoga 69
Scalping 131
Secession 138, 139, 155
Secretary of War 74
Sectional Hostilities 138, 153, 154
Securities market 90
Settling 26
Seward, William 167
Slave-hunters 146
Slave rebellions 150, 151
Slavery 34, 99, 100, 142, 154
Slave territory 157
Slave trade triangle 30
Slogans 57
Smith, Adam 85, 86
Smith, John 28
Social Capitalism 187
Social contracts 24
Socialism 187
Social Offspring 16
South 154, 155
South Carolina 140, 155
Southern capitalism 33, 98, 140, 142
Spain 43, 117, 118, 126
Spanish Armada 11
Speculators 83, 125
Squanto 27
Stamp Act 37, 55

State conventions 95
State power 120
States rights 80, 81, 97, 98
Status quo 22, 31
Stevens, Thaddeus 174
Subconscious inclinations 111
Suffering 147
Sugar Act 37, 55
Sumner, Charles 174
Sycophants 22
System 116
Tea Act 37
Tainos 10
Taney, Roger 156
Tariffs 139
Tarred and feathered 146
Taxation 162
Tennessee 132
Terrorists 179
Texas 134, 139
Thanksgiving 74
13th Amendment 171, 172, 174
3/4 ratification 100
3/5 provision 100, 157, 171, 177
Tobacco 28, 48, 51
Toussaint L'Ouverture 127
Tradition 16, 17
Traitor 63
Treasury Department 74
Treaty of Paris 69
Tyler, John 134
UndergroundRailroad 148

Underpaid labor 45, 51, 101, 135, 137
Uniform currency 82
United States 75, 116
Unpaid labor 32, 33, 46, 51, 121, 135, 137
Victory 68
Virginia 71
Vision 23
Vote 177
Wall Street 88-90, 160, 162, 188
War 60, 64, 89, 146, 147
War Between the States 54, 138, 152, 156
Washington, George 64, 68, 72, 110, 112, 117
Washitaw 41, 126, 127, 129
Wat Tyler 31
Wealth 135, 136, 137
Wealth of Nations 87, 88
Westward expansion 124, 134
Whiskey Rebellion 138
White mythology 19, 120, 133, 145, 189
White reality 145
Wisconsin 139
Women 28
Wool 27, 31